Ancients to
Middle Ages

Great Battles for Boys

By Joe Giorello

Ancients to Middle Ages
Great Battles for Boys

Copyright © 2018 Joe Giorello
Print Edition

All images are courtesy of the public domain, unless otherwise noted.
Maps of Western Mediterranean 264 BC & The Siege of Alesia by Jon Platek, Besvo
via Wikimedia Commons

Table of Contents

FOREWORD

IN ANCIENT TIMES, warfare was a way of life.

Men went into battle to settle almost every kind of conflict—from land and religion to politics and culture. Warfare was so important that most ancient political leaders were also military commanders, such as Julius Caesar.

The twelve battles in this book begin in the ancient world, which is the beginning of Western civilization, and move into the Middle Ages. You will learn about great empires that rose and fell, powerful kings that lived and died, and how the world we know today began developing—at the tip of a spear.

The Battle of Thermopylae

480 BC

Ancient Greek pottery showing Greek soldiers

YOU'VE PROBABLY HEARD THE TERM "last stand." For instance, people will say, "They made a brave last stand."

Last stand is a military phrase. It describes soldiers in a defensive position who realize they can't win the battle, but instead of surrendering, they choose to keep fighting—to their death. The battle is their "last stand."

History overflows with many amazing last-stand battles. One of the first last stands took place more than 2,000 years ago at the Battle of Thermopylae. (By the way, Thermopylae is pronounced "thur-mah-pill-eye." In Greek, it means "Gates of Fire.")

During ancient times, the Persian Empire ruled more than half of the known world. Look at the map. The Persians controlled all the territory inside that dark line. Now look toward the south (bottom of the map) and find an area marked Persia. That was the empire's home base.

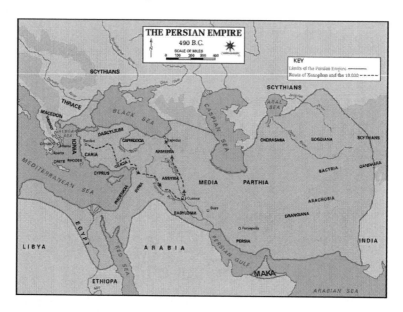

Now look over to the map's west side (left). Find Macedon and Ionia, which are outside that darkest line. These places, along with some outlying islands, were controlled by Ancient Greece. But the Persians wanted that territory, too, so they launched two military invasions.

The first Persian invasion, in 490 BC, failed.

But ten years later, in 480 BC, Persian King Xerxes launched the second invasion. Xerxes was determined to succeed. He amassed an army of men—some historians estimate Xerxes may have had one million men! Among his forces were 10,000 "Immortals," an elite heavy infantry force used for frontal assaults and anchoring defensive lines.

Xerxes also gathered together a navy of 1,200 ships. The ships were called triremes and were powered by huge sails and three levels of oarsmen ("tri" meaning "three"). Onboard the ship, a drummer pounded out a steady beat to keep the rowers synchronized. The rowing was backbreaking work because the triremes were so large. Consider this: an average modern automobile weighs about two tons. An average ancient trireme weighed about *forty* tons.

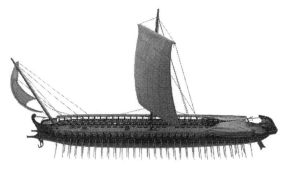

Trireme

While these triremes sailed for Greece, Xerxes marched his massive army across the Persian Empire and into northern Greece. He crushed all opponents. His next plan was to turn his forces south and conquer Athens, a powerful Greek city-state. Back then, there was only one route into Athens from northern Greece—through Thermopylae, the Gates of Fire.

Look at the next map. It shows Xerxes' invasion routes by land and sea into Greece. Over to the west (left) side, find Thessaly. Just below that is Thermopylae, a steep mountain pass.

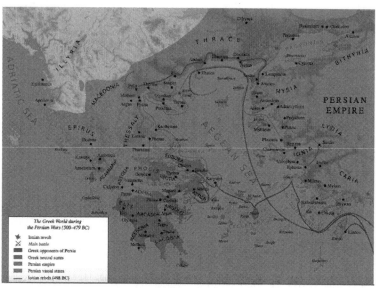

Map courtesy of Bibi Saint-Pol

This mountain pass was even more treacherous for Xerxes because Spartan warriors were on the other side, waiting for the Persians.

If the Immortals were the Persians' elite fighting force, the Spartans were the Greeks' *ultra*-elite force. As boys, Spartans were taken from their families and forced to live in military barracks. They spent the rest of their lives learning how to fight and win battles. The Spartans lived for war.

Spartan King Leonidas was encamped at Thermopylae with 300 Spartan soldiers and 5,000 regular Greek soldiers. The Spartans were recognizable by their distinctive uniforms. They wore red cloaks, bronze helmets, bronze breastplates, and bronze greaves to protect their lower legs. Spartans also carried an innovative shield called a hoplon. It was larger than most shields and curved outward. The hoplon allowed the Spartan warriors to line up in formation and push back against enemy lines while protecting their own men on either side. Other Spartan weapons included a six- to eight-foot thrusting spear that had an iron shaft at one end and a bronze butt-spike at the other, and a two-foot-long double-edged sword whose blade widened toward the tip.

Spartan Warrior

King Leonidas chose to meet Xerxes' invasion at Thermopylae for strategic reasons. The Persian forces greatly outnumbered the Greeks—by as much as fifty to one. But Thermopylae's narrow mountain path would only allow so many men through at one time. Leonidas' men probably wouldn't have to fight all the Persians at once.

Xerxes didn't want to face the Spartans this soon. He planned to conquer Athens, then force those Greeks to fight on his side. Xerxes waited several days at Thermopylae, hoping the Spartans would leave. But the Spartans stayed, and Xerxes realized he had no choice but to fight them if he wanted to reach Athens.

First, Xerxes ordered his archers to fire a barrage of arrows at Leonidas' forces. But the Spartans deflected that volley with their hoplon shields.

Next, Xerxes sent in his infantry. These Persian soldiers had won many of their battles by smashing into their enemy and creating panic in the lines. But Leonidas' men didn't break, in part because the Spartans used a phalanx formation. The phalanx was four men deep and eight men across—a literal human wall!

At first, the massive numbers of Persian soldiers were winning against Leonidas' forces, but then the bronze wall of Spartans dug in and pushed back. Using their long spears to draw blood, the Spartans penetrated deep into the ranks of the Persians. Then the swords came out. Slashing and stabbing, the Spartans left the Persians to die on the battlefield. More and more blood spilled as the Spartan machine moved forward, stepping over the dead and wounded.

Realizing this was no regular enemy, the Persians retreated.

In ancient times, warfare was brutal and intense. But the close clashes didn't usually last long—probably less than one minute each. During this one attack, however, the Greeks killed more than 1,000 Persians.

Ancient Greek phalanx

On the second day of battle, Xerxes sent in the Immortals.

But the Spartans only shouted war cries and taunted the enemy to come closer. When the Immortals finally struck, the Spartans held their ground using their short swords for close-combat killing. The Immortals who survived this fight had to stumble back to camp over thousands of dead bodies.

Spartan battles were terrifying. Soldiers were sometimes given rations of wine *before* the battle broke out because so many soldiers would die or become disfigured. With that high casualty rate, the Spartans invented an early version of dog tags. Before the battle, soldiers would snap a twig and leave one-half in camp and tie to the other half to their wrist. If a soldier died on the battlefield, his fellow soldiers could remove the wrist-twig, bring it back to camp, and match it to the other half to identify him.

At Thermopylae, the outnumbered Spartans were winning.

But on the battle's third day, a Greek traitor reached Xerxes and told the Persian king about another route into Athens. It was a little-known goat path that went around Thermopylae. Now Xerxes could move his forces around the Spartans—and sneak up from behind.

From the beginning of this battle, Leonidas may have realized it was a suicide mission—one of those last stands. His forces were heavily outnumbered, and no reinforcements were coming. That knowledge may explain why on the third day of battle, Leonidas sent away most of his soldiers, keeping only his 300 Spartans and some well-trained Greeks.

Then the Persians snuck up on Leonidas. Xerxes demanded the Spartans surrender their weapons.

Leonidas replied, "Come and take them."

Xerxes then threatened to fire so many arrows it would blot out the sun.

"This is pleasant news," replied one Spartan warrior, "for if the Persians hide the sun, we shall have our battle in the shade."

Xerxes attacked them from all sides. The Spartan phalanx held—at first—but the battle soon descended into close-quarter combat with short swords. Leonidas' men killed thousands of Persians. But Xerxes' archers kept firing—Xerxes didn't even care if the arrows hit his own forces, as long as he won this battle—and one arrow hit Leonidas, killing him.

The Persian soldiers raced forward, overtook the Spartans, and slaughtered them all.

The Battle of Thermopylae was over. The Persians had won.

But even in death, the Spartans could claim some victories.

Even though outnumbered, they killed thousands of Xerxes men. The hard fight also slowed down the invasion of Athens. And while Xerxes fought the Spartans at that steep mountain pass, his triremes off the coast of Athens were getting hammered by violent storms. Hundreds of Persian ships sank. Finally, when Xerxes' forces managed to arrive in Athens, most of the city had already fled, having heard about the Spartans at Thermopylae. In response, Xerxes burned Athens to the ground.

Now the Persian king turned his sights his next great battle: the island of Salamis.

WHO FOUGHT?

Statue of King Leonidas

Spartan boys grew up to be soldiers—only soldiers. Every other job in Sparta was done by slaves.

At around age seven, Spartan boys were sent to military schools and never lived at home again. Barracks life was extremely difficult—on purpose. For instance, boys were given only small rations of food so that they would get hungry enough to steal. Being able to steal food was a valuable skill for soldiers inside enemy territory. To hone their thievery even further, the boys were beaten if they were caught stealing—not for stealing but for getting caught!

Spartan philosophy can be summed up by some of their sayings. Here are a few:

"He who sweats more in training bleeds less in war."

"A city is well-fortified which has a wall of men instead of brick."

"Come back with your shield—or on it."

By age twenty, Spartan men were full-time soldiers. They remained on active duty until they were sixty years old, pledging their loyalty to the military and their fellow soldiers. Spartans also developed strong excellent character traits such as courage and self-control. That discipline made them deadly on the battlefield.

After the Persians killed King Leonidas in the Battle of Thermopylae, they paraded his body around Greece as a trophy—and a warning to anyone who might resist Xerxes' invasion.

But later, the Spartans retrieved Leonidas' remains and built a shrine in his honor.

BOOKS

300 Heroes: The Battle of Thermopylae (Capstone Press)

Leonidas: Hero of Thermopylae by Ian McGregor Morris

INTERNET

The History Channel online offers several excellent videos about the Battle of Thermopylae, including one about Spartan weapons and battle formations: www.history.com/topics/ancient-history/leonidas/videos/spartans-implements-of-death

MOVIES

The 300 Spartans (1962). The 2006 remake of this movie is rated R.

The Battle of Salamis

September 23, 480 BC

BATTLE OF SALAMIS.

WHILE XERXES FOUGHT the Spartans at Thermopylae, his triremes were sinking off the coast of Athens. He lost half his fleet, leaving him with only 600 triremes.

But the Greek navy was in even worse shape. It had only 200 triremes. Now, with Xerxes headed for Athens, those ships sailed to a nearby island named Salamis.

Look at the map. Dotted lines show the Greek triremes leaving Athens, and the path taken by Greek troops marching over land—all trying to escape Persian invasion forces. You can see the location of Thermopylae in the middle of the map. Below that, find the island of Salamis.

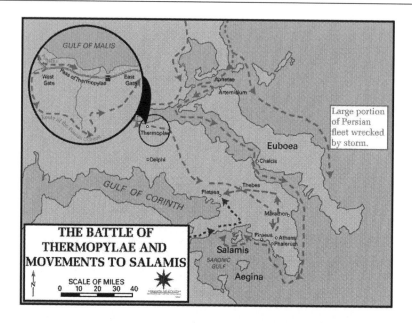

The Persians expected a quick victory at Salamis. After all, they'd beaten the Spartans at Thermopylae, overtaken Athens, burned that mighty city to the ground, and still had three times as many ships as the Greeks. Moreover, the Persians were more experienced sailors than the Greeks. With all this in his favor, Xerxes felt confident—so confident that he decided to watch this battle from a nearby hillside.

Persian King Xerxes watches the battle from a hillside

Triremes used several tactics in battle. One tactic involved the ship's prow—the front end. It was equipped with a bronze battering ram that could smash into an enemy's wooden ship, tear open a giant hole, and sink the entire vessel, usually drowning the whole crew, too.

A second tactic was to sail so closely to an enemy trireme that their oars snapped off, disabling the ship.

A third tactic was called boarding. Once a ship was disabled, sailors would jump onboard and fight in hand-to-hand combat.

Greek trireme ramming Persian trireme, followed by boarding.

But for all these tactics to work, commanders need to be able to communicate with their sailors. Xerxes had conquered many foreign enemies, shifting them into his forces. Those men didn't speak Persian and couldn't understand battlefield orders. Naval commanders resorted to standing on the main ship's bow and giving orders with trumpet calls and flags. But once the fighting broke out, those signals were drowned out by all the yelling, screaming, and splashing. For that reason, it was crucial to have a clear battle plan *before* the actual battle began.

The Persians' plan heading into the Battle of Salamis was to form three lines of ships. These lines would sail into a narrow channel off Salamis, one right behind the other.

Look at the next map. It shows the Persians in this three-line formation off Salamis. Notice, too, how the Greek ships are lined up defensively against the island, almost as if trapped there.

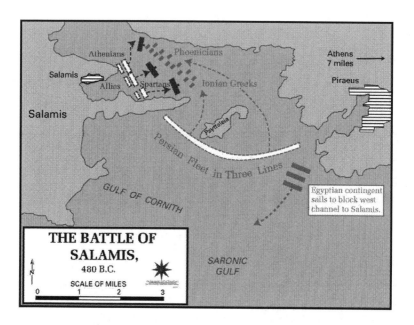

But before the battle started, something unexpected happened. Some Greek prisoners of war escaped from the Persians and ran back to their countrymen. They revealed the Persians' plan to amass all those triremes in that narrow channel off Salamis, so many ships the Greek fleet couldn't escape. They'd either have to surrender or die.

The situation looked grim.

But thanks to a brilliant naval commander, the Greeks came up with a counterattack. The commander's name was Themistocles.

Themistocles decided they wouldn't try to stop the Persian ships coming into the channel. Nor would they try to escape.

Instead, the Greek ships would hold their positions. Stay put. Let the Persians come.

So the Greeks watched as the Persian ships sailed closer. And closer. The Persian ships clogged the entire channel. No Greek ship could ever escape. Xerxes, watching this from that hillside, probably saw certain victory.

That's when Themistocles launched his attack.

Sailing straight at the Persians, the Greeks rammed their brass prows into the wooden hulls. The Persian triremes tried to maneuver out of the way but they couldn't. Too many ships were crammed into that narrow bay—and more vessels were lined up behind them.

As the ships sank, Xerxes' sailors fell overboard and drowned.

But Themistocles wasn't done. He ordered his ships to find any openings in the Persian lines. As some of the Greeks slipped through, they circled behind the Persians and attacked from the rear.

Now the boarding parties leaped onto the Persian triremes. Sailors swung swords, stabbed spears, and slaughtered their invaders. On land, the Greek soldiers began destroying the Persian army.

The Greeks won the Battle of Salamis—in a rout.

Now Xerxes was facing new problems. It was already September, winter was coming, and his damaged forces were running low on supplies. Xerxes decided to abandon this invasion, withdrawing the bulk of his army. But he left behind a small contingent of forces, hoping to come back and conquer the Greeks. The following year, however, the Greeks once again defeated the Persians. Xerxes finally withdrew all his forces.

The Battle of Salamis won freedom for Greece. And later, it would prove to be the battle that stopped the Persian Empire from expanding into the rest of the known world. Today, it's considered one of the most significant naval battles of all time.

WHO FOUGHT?

Bust of Themisocles

During the time Xerxes was marching his invasion force toward Greece, Themistocles was one of Athens' most prominent politicians and he persuaded the Athenians to build a naval fleet to fight the Persians. Those same ships were used to win the Battle of Salamis.

After Salamis, Themistocles was considered a hero. Unfortunately, fame made him arrogant and turned him into a lousy leader who was eventually sent into exile—banished from Greece. The Spartans even wanted to kill Themistocles, believing he was part of a treasonous plot against one of their generals. In exile, Themistocles traveled all the way into the Persian Empire.

And that's where history took one of its strangest turns.

You'd think the Persians would want to kill Themistocles for defeating them at Salamis. Instead, Themistocles started serving under King Artaxerxes I—the son of Xerxes!—and rose through the Persian ranks.

How is that possible?

There's an old saying, "The enemy of my enemy is my friend."

The Persians hated the Greeks. And the Greeks now hated Themistocles. That made Themistocles an enemy of Persia's enemy—or a "friend" of Persia.

For the rest of his life, Themistocles lived in the Persian Empire. It was only much later, after historians evaluated his role in the Battle of Salamis, that his reputation was restored to hero status in the Western world.

Today, Themistocles is considered a tactical naval genius.

BOOKS

The Battle of Salamis by Charles River Editors

Salamis 480 BC: The naval campaign that saved Greece by William Shepherd

The Greatest Battles of the Greco-Persian Wars: Marathon, Thermopylae, and Salamis by Charles River Editors

INTERNET

"The Persian Wars in 5 Minutes":
youtube.com/watch?v=jMlnn7hKBn0

MOVIES

The 300 Spartans (1962) Although the movie focuses on the Battle of Thermopylae, Themistocles is one of the main characters.

The Battle of Issus

333 BC

Ancient rendering of the Battle of Issus. Alexander the Great rides horseback
(far left). King Darius rides the chariot.

BY STOPPING THE PERSIAN INVASION, Greece won peace.

It was the kind of peace that would change the world. Since they didn't have to be fighting Persia, the Greek city-states could focus on their own citizens. Architects began designing buildings without worrying that invaders would burn them to the ground. Historians had time to record events—including what we know about battles such as Thermopylae and Salamis. Philosophers developed new ideas, including a philosopher named Hippocrates who wrote down rules for doctors which today's doctors still follow by taking their Hippocratic Oath. And finally, a brand-new form of government appeared—democracy. In peace, civilization leaped forward.

But throughout the history of mankind, peace has never lasted.

In 336 BC, an assassin murdered the king of northern Grece, an area known as Macedonia. The king's son took over the throne. His name was Alexander. But it wasn't long before he was known as Alexander the Great, one of history's greatest military leaders.

One of King Philip's accomplishments was to unite all the Greek city-states into one country. Two years later, Philip was assassinated, and Alexander started his invasion of the Persian Empire.

Look at the map. It shows Alexander's invasion forces leaving Macedonia in the north (upper left) and pushing into Persian territory.

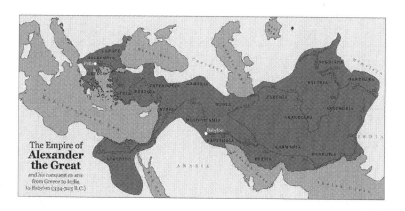

Persian King Darius III wanted to stop Alexander's invasion.

Darius had an army of about 100,000 men. Most of his soldiers were light infantry or horseback soldiers, known as cavalry. Darius also had some heavy cavalry—soldiers riding horses who carried large shields and swords—and the highly trained Immortals.

Alexander had several disadvantages. His army numbered only about 30,000 men, and they were far from home. So not only did the Persians have a three to one advantage, but they knew the territory better than the Greeks and could count on help from friendly civilians.

With so many disadvantages going into this invasion, most military leaders would have abandoned it. But Alexander the Great only moved his forces deeper and deeper into Persian territory.

Alexander the Great leading his forces in battle

Darius didn't expect such bold action. In fact, his entire battle plan revolved around the Greeks retreating. But someone who knew Alexander warned Darius: "He will make all the speed he can to meet you, and is now most likely on his march toward you."

Darius was known for being ruthless. He'd won the throne by poisoning a king—then he turned around and gave the poison to the same man who helped him kill that king. Now this vicious Persian ruler was determined to kill Alexander the Great.

Darius marched his forces to Issus near the Mediterranean Sea. You can find Issus on the previous map, located on the sea's east coast (right side of map).

On their way to fight Alexander, the Persian army captured some Greeks. Darius made an example of them. He cut off their hands and paraded these prisoners around the area, showing everyone what would happen if they disobeyed the king or took the Greeks' side in this invasion.

King Darius

When Alexander's cavalry scouts heard about these prisoners of war, they rode back to warn him. Darius was on the warpath with a huge army. Meanwhile, the Greeks had no reinforcements.

Alexander continued to push ahead, sending out his cavalry units to secure his forward route and scout for Darius' exact location.

But Darius was doing something very clever. He knew Alexander expected him to lead his Persian army through the area's easiest routes. Instead, Darius was marching his forces through the rugged Syrian mountains. And by doing that, he managed to sneak up on the Greeks at Issus and cut off their supply lines.

Now Alexander was outnumbered three to one in enemy territory with his enemy strategically surrounding him and blocking the sources of food and water. As if that wasn't enough at Issus, Darius placed his highly skilled Persian cavalry on flat land, facing Alexander's right flank. On the other flank, Darius placed 80,000 light infantry soldiers. His heavy infantry stood dead-center, and Darius was among them.

Could things get any worse for Alexander?

Yes.

Alexander's soldiers wore bronze helmets and bronze breastplates. In the hot climate of the Middle East, the metal overheated their heads and bodies. Meanwhile, the Persian soldiers wore little more than cloth tunics and carried light spears and shields made from stretched animal skins.

At this point, the Battle of Issus looked like an easy win for the Persians.

Alexander had studied military tactics from a young age. He had also trained his infantry to use The Box, a formation similar to the Spartan's phalanx. Alexander's Box was sixteen men deep. Its forward soldiers were armed with long spears—some of them as long as eighteen feet—while behind them even stronger men pushed forward. The Box was a deadly force on the battlefield. With his cavalry on the flanks, Alexander knew how to coordinate his attacks.

When Darius launched an attack across a river at Issus, Alexander counterattacked with The Box. His men shoved the Persian soldiers all the way back across the river—then kept going, slaughtering the enemy as they went. Darius' lines broke, and Alexander's cavalry galloped through the holes, slashing their way through the ranks, continuing until they passed the Persian camp. hen Alexander wheeled his forces around and captured the camp. Darius realized he could be captured or killed. He fled the battlefield. Seeing his retreat, his troops suddenly realized the battle was lost. A rout ensued.

The Battle for Issus was over.

Alexander the Great had beaten the Persians while outnumbered three to one, inside the Persians' own territory, and with his supplies cut off He also captured their king.

The battle claimed about 6,000 Greeks, dead and wounded. But Darius lost almost his entire army—some 80,000 men. After the battle, Alexander walked into Darius' tent. Even during military campaigns, the Persian king lived in great luxury. Silk carpets covered the floor of his tent. Drinks were served in bejeweled vessels. Servants and slaves abounded. Alexander, on the other hand, lived with only the bare necessities of a military commander fighting on a battlefield. Looking around Darius' tent, Alexander said, "So this is what it means to be a king."

After the Battle of Issus, Alexander continued his invasion of the Persian Empire. Within several years, he had conquered most of the known world and destroyed what remained of that once-great empire.

WHO FOUGHT?

Statue of Alexander the Great

Alexander the Great was a bright and ambitious boy. His father, King Philip of Macedon, once told him, "My boy, you must find a kingdom big enough for your ambition. Macedon is too small for you."

Alexander's warrior training began at age seven—much like a Spartan. He learned to ride horses and fight with swords. When Alexander was thirteen, his father hired Aristotle, a famous Greek philosopher, as the boy's tutor. Aristotle schooled Alexander in everything from science and math to philosophy and poetry. Combined with his warrior training, that intellectual knowledge made Alexander an exceptionally smart military leader.

Alexander began going on military expeditions as a teenager, when his father was king and leading the Macedon army. Alexander soon earned command of a cavalry unit. When he was twenty years old, his father was assassinated. Alexander assumed the throne.

During his reign, Alexander traveled more than 20,000 miles on horseback. He conquered the kingdoms of Persia, Babylon, and significant parts of Asia. Eventually, Alexander the Great controlled most of the known world.

In 323 BC, while on a military campaign, Alexander came down with a severe fever. Historians suspect he caught pneumonia or contracted malaria—a virus spread by mosquitos.

Several days after the fever began, Alexander died.

He was thirty-two years old.

***

One quick note before we go any further.

You may have noticed that the years of these BC battles are counting downward in time. For instance, the Battle of Thermopylae took place in 480 BC. The Battle of Issus, more than 100 years later, happened in 333 BC. Shouldn't the dates being going up in number?

Here's what's happening.

Ancient historical dates are known as BC, which stands for for "Before Christ." The dates move downward from, say, year 5000 BC to year 1. That year marks the birth of Jesus Christ. After his birth, dates begin counting upward. These years are labeled "AD," which stands for *Anno Domini,* a Latin phrase meaning "in the year of our Lord."

BOOKS

The Life of Alexander the Great (Stories From History) by Dr. Nicholas Saunders (Author)

Alexander the Great by Demi

Alexander the Great: Master of the Ancient World (Wicked History) by Doug Wilhelm

INTERNET

Eight Surprising Facts about Alexander the Great:
www.history.com/news/history-lists/eight-surprising-facts-
about-alexander-the-great

MOVIES

Alexander the Great (1956)

Battle of Cannae Second Punic Wars

216 BC

Hannibal's war elephants

THE EMPIRES OF PERSIA AND GREECE dominated the ancient world, but as the BC years were counting downward, another realm was rising—Rome.

Smart, reliable, and ruthless warriors, the Romans would eventually control even more territory than Alexander the Great. The empire would also have many emperors—some admirable, some terrible—but each one wanted to grow the empire's power and wealth. That growth required near-constant military campaigns.

However, invasions and wars cost money—so much money that countries sometimes went bankrupt fighting battles.

That's what happened in the Punic Wars.

The word "punic" comes from a Latin term to describe people who lived in Carthage, a powerful Greek city-state. The Punic Wars pitted Carthage against Rome. These wars were among the longest conflicts in human history, lasting more than 100 years.

Look at the map. It shows several different civilizations around the western Mediterranean in the year 264 BC. Notice Italy—it's shaped like a boot—and Italy's capital city of Rome. That was home base of the Roman Empire.

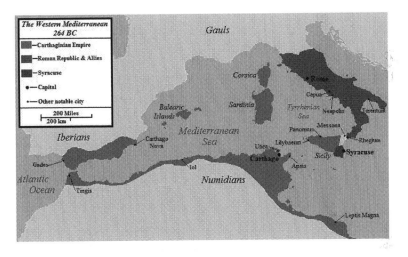

Now look at Italy's "toe." You will see some islands near that coastline—specifically Sicily, Sardinia, and Corsica. These islands hug Italy's coast but Carthage had control over them, even though the rest of Carthage was across the Mediterranean Sea and into parts of North Africa.

The Romans wanted these islands, so they launched a war against Carthage.

That was the First Punic War. Rome won and took over the islands.

During the war, Carthage used mercenaries. Mercenaries are soldiers with no loyalty to any particular country; they fight because that's what they're paid to do. The price for these mercenaries, among other expenses of war, bankrupted Carthage. When the government couldn't pay the soldiers, the soldiers launched a siege on the city of Carthage itself.

One man saved Carthage from destruction. His name was Hamilcar Barca. A military leader during the First Punic War, Hamilcar was greatly admired because he fought bravely alongside his soldiers. But when Hamilcar died, the fate of Carthage seemed uncertain until his son rose to power.

His name was Hannibal.

Hannibal would overshadow his father's reputation and become one of the most effective military leaders of all time. Hannibal also wanted to exact revenge on Rome, and that desire helped launch the Second Punic War.

War Elephants in battle

Hannibal built up a large army. It included hundreds of African war elephants. In the year 218 BC, Hannibal marched this force toward Rome. This trek is considered one of history's greatest military feats because it involved thousands upon thousands of men, weapons, food, water, other supplies, and the elephants, all of it crossing the Italian Alps, some of the highest and steepest mountains in the entire world.

Look at the next map. The dotted line represents Hannibal's invasion route beginning in southern Spain, which belonged to Carthage, and into Italy.

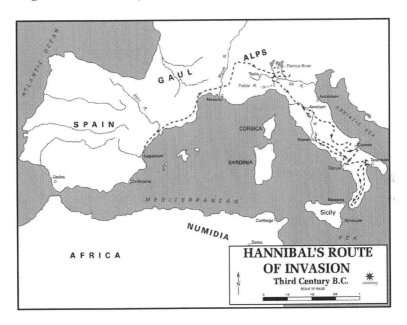

By late 218 BC, Hannibal's army was defeating the Roman forces inside the empire and gaining more soldiers. The Romans were generally wicked rulers. For instance, Roman tax collectors demanded a lot of money from people, and they harshly punished any lawbreakers, especially those refusing to pay taxes. The Romans even invented new forms of torture, such as crucifixion in which a man was nailed to a cross while still alive then left hanging there until he died. To fight back against the Romans, people were joining Hannibal's army.

And Hannibal was winning. In the early summer of 217 BC, Hannibal's men were hiding in a wooded area near some Roman soldiers. Hannibal told his men to light campfires in the woods. When the Roman soldiers saw the smoke, they thought they could sneak up on Hannibal's forces. Instead, Hannibal's men sprang on them and killed them.

Later that summer, Hannibal fought in his most famous battle. It happened at Cannae, a city located just above Italy's "heel."

Hannibal's army crossing the Alps

A Roman commander named Varro was at Cannae with about 90,000 men—nearly twice as many soldiers as Hannibal.

Varro vowed to stop Hannibal's invasion.

Hannibal, however, was going to set another trap, even better than the campfire smoke.

His first ploy involved positioning.

Hannibal placed his army at Cannae with their backs against a river. Since waterways limit an army's ability to maneuver, this position looked foolish. Water also hindered any retreat or escape. But this was summer in southern Italy—very hot—and Hannibal knew his men would need water. He'd also studied the wind's movement, and how it blew across this terrain. With his men positioned near the water, Hannibal knew that when the battle broke out, the wind would blow the dust into the Romans' faces.

Hannibal used more traditional placements for his cavalry, with the horse soldiers on the wings. But his cavalry included some exceptional riders known as the Numidians. These bareback riders wore no heavy armor and galloped across battlefields hurling javelins with deadly accuracy. These riders were on Hannibal's right wing.

On his left wing, Hannibal positioned his heavy cavalry, mostly European riders who were wealthy enough to afford chain mail—shirts made of protective metal mesh—and who carried swords and shields. In the center of this battle formation, Hannibal placed his infantry soldiers which included some Spanish fighters brandishing large oval shields and other weapons, from spears and javelins to thrusting swords.

But it was Hannibal's next choice that made this battle legendary.

He ordered his forces into a crescent-shaped formation.

When Varro launched his attack, Hannibal ordered the center of the crescent to hold their position, while the flanks on either side surged forward to attack the enemy. These wing soldiers raced at the Roman cavalry, yanking the riders from their mounts and killing them. Varro's force fled from the battlefield. But the fight wasn't over.

Look at the next map. It shows Hannibal's crescent-shaped battle formation. Notice the wings and center. Now follow the arrows. Near the top, the arrows show Hannibal's cavalry attacking the Roman cavalry—before Hannibal's riders got *behind* the Roman infantry lines and attacked from that position, too. Yet the whole time, that crescent's center held the line, and even moved back, letting the Romans come forward.

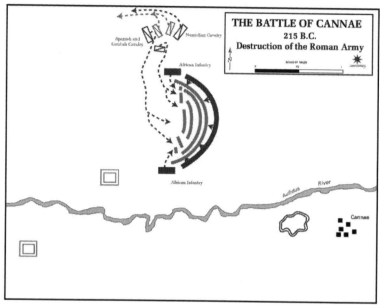

Battle map with crescent

As the Romans surged into Hannibal's center, Varro felt even more confident of victory. Not only did he have twice as many men as Hannibal, his soldiers weren't tired—they hadn't crossed the Alps and trekked down the length of Italy.

Then the crescent began to collapse. With each step forward, the Romans thought they were defeating Hannibal.

But in reality, Hannibal's men were giving up ground on purpose. Brilliantly, Hannibal was using his enemy's own progress against itself! And then, like a gate slamming shut behind a herd of animals, Hannibal ordered his flanks to close around the enemy. A wave of panic shot through the Romans—they were surrounded! No escape was possible.

In most of Hannibal's battles, he typically took prisoners at this point, and later used them to fight against his enemies. But at Cannae, no prisoners were taken.

The battlefield turned into a bloodbath. Swords slashed, slicing off arms and legs. Spears sank deep into men's chests. Heads were cut from bodies. This slaughter became so horrific that Roman soldiers began digging holes in the ground and shoving their faces into the dirt, hoping to suffocate themselves before Hannibal's men could kill them.

The Battle of Cannae claimed 50,000 lives, almost all of them Roman.

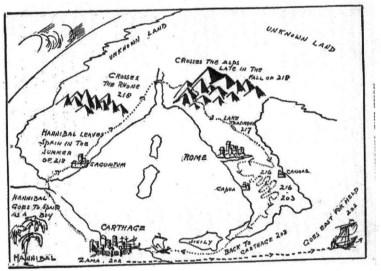

Hand-drawn map

Outnumbered, deep inside enemy territory, his men exhausted, Hannibal had won the Battle of Cannae by outwitting the Romans with his crescent maneuver.

To this day, military leaders study Hannibal's tactics. In fact, more than two thousand years after Hannibal used that crescent maneuver, United States General Norman Schwarzkopf defeated the Iraqi army—and credited his swift victory to Hannibal's crescent.

But after winning the Battle of Cannae, Hannibal was forced out of Italy. The Roman armies cleverly began attacking

Carthage's outer territories, forcing Hannibal to leave Italy and protect those lands. Meanwhile, this Second Punic War would continue another thirty years.

And in the end, Rome would win—again.

WHO FOUGHT?

Hannibal (249-183 B.C.), the great Carthaginian general and statesman. A bust showing him in later life. National Museum, Naples.

Hannibal

Hannibal Barca is considered one of the forefathers of military strategy. Using sly tactics and cunning maneuvers, Hannibal regularly defeated armies much larger than his own.

As a young boy, Hannibal begged his father to let him fight on the battlefield. Hamilcar agreed, on one condition: Hannibal must never become a friend of Rome.

Hannibal told his father, "I will use fire and steel to arrest the destiny of Rome."

After his father's death, Hannibal didn't immediately assume control of Carthage. His brother-in-law took command of the Carthaginian army, and Hannibal was serving as an army officer. But when his brother-in-law was assassinated, Hannibal took charge.

After fighting in the Second Punic War, Hannibal became a statesman and served in government. But he continued to lead military campaigns, seizing every opportunity to harass Rome. Eventually, the Romans got so sick of Hannibal that they demanded his surrender. Instead, Hannibal chose voluntary exile, though he later returned to battle—he just couldn't stop attacking the Romans!

Finally, the Romans ordered his death.

However, nobody's sure exactly how Hannibal died.

One legend says Hannibal was wounded while riding his horse and later died of an infection. Another legend—probably the most accepted—says Hannibal didn't want the Romans to have the honor of killing him, so he took his own life, ingesting poison he kept in his ring.

BOOKS

Famous Men Of Rome: History for the Thoughtful Child by John H. Haaren and A. B. Poland

Hannibal: Rome's Worst Nightmare (Wicked History) by Philip Brooks

The Romans: Usborne Illustrated World History by Graham Tingay and Anthony Marks

The Young Carthaginian by G. A. Henty

INTERNET

"Ten Things You Should Know About the Battle of Cannae": www.realmofhistory.com/2016/06/07/10-facts-battle-of-cannae

YouTube offers several good video clips showing reenactments of the Battle of Cannae.

The Battle of Alesia The Gallic Wars

52 BC

Vercingetorix surrendering to Julius Caesar

YOU'VE PROBABLY HEARD OF JULIUS CAESAR, the famous Roman emperor. But you might not know that Julius Caesar was also a great military leader.

One of his most legendary battles took place in 52 BC at the Battle of Alesia.

In its quest for more territory, the Roman Empire launched many invasions and battles in places that today we recognize as Europe—France, Germany, Belgium, etc. These battles in Europe were known as The Gallic Wars. Within five years of launching this campaign, the Roman army had conquered most of France.

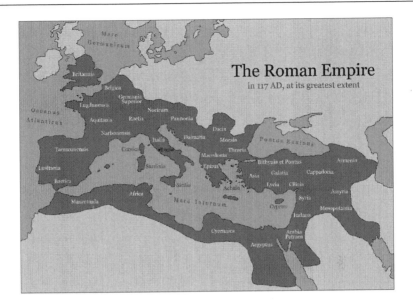

The Gallic tribes in Europe realized they needed a military leader strong enough, and clever enough, to stop the Romans. They chose a man named Vercingetorix (pronounced Ver-SING-A-tore-icks).

Vercingetorix united the tribes and built up a military force of about 150,000 men—nearly twice as many as Julius' 75,000 soldiers. But Vercingetorix knew that the two-to-one advantage wasn't enough. This battle against Rome would require careful planning, cunning strategies, and a secure location.

One artist's depiction of Vercingetorix

For the battlefield's location, Vercingetorix chose a hilltop in France called Alesia. It was high ground, which made a good defensive position since both horses and men struggle to run uphill. Alesia also had two rivers that ran on either side of the hill, further hindering an attack. Finally, France was friendly territory for the Gallic tribes.

Next, Vercingetorix ordered his men to cut down the trees and build a wooden stockade, or fence, with towers. This fence ran around the hilltop, adding another defensive layer.

When Julius and his army arrived in Alesia, they realized the Gauls' excellent position. Hills, rivers, and walls—it would be almost impossible to attack that position. Any other military commander might've launched a barrage of arrows or catapulted boulders, or tried to tear down the fence.

But Julius built his own fence. It was twelve feet high and ran for miles—miles!—around the hill. Julius planned to lock the Gauls inside their own fortifications, then starve them into surrendering.

Romans building the walls and trenches around Alesia

Vercingetorix suddenly realized Julius' plan. He decided to attack before that wall could be completed. These first assaults didn't break the Roman lines, but one cavalry unit managed to slip through, racing to gather reinforcements.

Julius ordered his men to dig a trench around the wall. This trench was twenty feet deep! Consider this: Modern ceilings usually are about eight feet high. Double that distance, add four feet, and you're at the depth of this trench. After that trench was dug, Julius ordered his soldiers to dig *two more* trenches—each one fifteen feet deep—and fill one with water from the rivers. He created a moat.

Part of Vercingetorix's plan was still working. He had pinned the Romans to one location, forcing them to find food and other supplies in enemy territory. And that was difficult because the local people didn't like the Romans.

But when Vercingetorix's cavalry returned with a relief force, Julius built *another* wall! This one ran around his own forces, protecting them from outside attacks. Basically, the Romans were now camping between two walls. To further protect his men, Julius ordered them to add sharpened spears to the wall's outer side.

Look at the map. It shows some of these walls around Alesia.

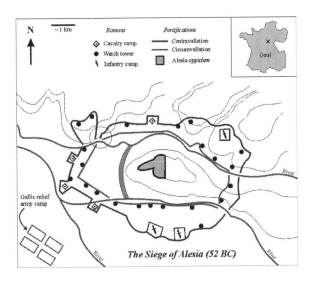

The Siege of Alesia (52 BC)

Vercingetorix knew that time was running out for the Gauls. His men could starve to death on that hilltop, or escape.

Vercingetorix decided it was time to attack the Romans again. This time, it would be a two-fold attack. One set of Gauls would strike the Roman's outer wall, while Vercingetorix's men attacked from inside, creating chaos and confusion for the Romans. Then Vercingetorix and his men could escape—and possibly kill some Romans as they fled.

But before that attack could be launched, a Roman military leader showed up with reinforcements. Although the Gauls still had more men than the Romans, this new military leader was another masterful strategist. His name was Marc Anthony.

When the Gauls attacked, Julius and Marc Anthony shifted their outnumbered forces from one place to another, continually meeting the most aggressive forces. But when the Roman lines threatened to break, Julius made a bold move.

He ordered more than 6,000 Roman cavalry soldiers to ride beyond the outer wall and circle back behind the Gauls on the outside. Now it was the outside Gallic force that was fighting men in a two-pronged battle. Realizing the Romans would soon have them completely surrounded, meaning certain death, the outer Gauls broke rank and ran. The Roman cavalry pursued them, killing hundreds of men.

The next day, Vercingetorix was still trapped inside those walls. He saw no way to win this battle at Alesia, and asked Julius for terms of surrender. Vercingetorix even offered to surrender himself if Julius would spare the lives of his men.

The Battle of Alesia was over.

Julius agreed to Vercingetorix's request, but with one condition. Vercingetorix must arrive in Rome wearing chains. Why? Because Julius was also a skilled politician. He knew the site of this humbled Gallic leader would only grow Julius' legend as a military leader.

The Gallic Wars continued for two more years, but the Gauls never gained an upper hand. Rome conquered the rest of Europe. They took more than one million Gauls as slaves, and killed roughly the same number.

Later, Julius became emperor of the Roman Empire.

WHO FOUGHT?

Julius Caesar

Julius Caesar was born around the year 100 BC. He came from an aristocratic family but, by Roman standards, his parents weren't wealthy. They were respected, however, and when Julius was about six years old, he began studying with a private tutor.

At age seventeen, Julius married the daughter of a powerful politician and joined the army. He proved to be a courageous military soldier on the battlefield, and when he returned to Rome, he quickly rose through the government, making friends with powerful and wealthy men.

At age forty, Julius was elected to consul—sort of like becoming president, but consuls only served one year. After his term, Julius became governor of the province of Gaul, leading four Roman legions and earning the reputation as one of Rome's best military leaders in battles such as Alesia.

The Roman people admired and supported Julius. But many politicians hated him, fearing he was becoming too popular. When Julius announced he would run for consul again, the Roman Senate demanded he first surrender command of his army. Julius refused. The Senate then labeled him a traitor.

In 49 BC, Julius marched toward Rome with his army, taking control of the city of Rome. He spent the next eighteen months battling his opposition. One of his worst enemies was a man named Pompey. Julius eventually chased Pompey all the way to Egypt—where the pharaoh killed Pompey and gave Julius the gift of Pompey's head.

Julius returned to Rome, the most powerful man in the world. His name was changed to Julius Caesar. "Caesar" was a title like "emperor" or "king." Other Roman rulers later added "Caesar" to their names, too.

Caesar made many changes to the Roman Empire, mostly for the better. He instituted reforms in government, particularly ways to help the poor, and he rebuilt much of the city of Rome. He also changed the calendar. Today we follow this Julian calendar that has 365 days and a leap year every four years. The calendar also includes the month of "July," named after Julius.

But not everyone was thrilled with Julius Caesar's leadership.

On March 15, in the year 44 BC, Julius Caesar walked into the Roman Senate. The senators attacked, stabbing him twenty-three times.

Julius Caesar died from the wounds.

BOOKS

History for Kids: The Illustrated Lives of Julius Caesar and Caesar Augustus by Charles River Editors

The Kingfisher Book of the Ancient World: From the Ice Age to the Fall of Rome by Hazel Mary Martell

INTERNET

An animated depiction of how the Roman and Gallic lines shifted around the walls in the Battle of Alesia: www.youtube.com/watch?v=SU1Ej9Yqt68, www.youtube.com/watch?v=lMFiED6sAi8

MOVIES

Vercingetorix (2001)

Battle of Jotapata

67 AD

The Jewish Revolt Against Rome

Roman soldiers assaulting a wall

ROME'S HARSH RULE CAUSED a lot of suffering. Among the people suffering most were the Jews living in Judea, which today is Israel.

The Romans first occupied Judea in the year 63 BC. With each year forward, and into the AD years, the Romans made life even more difficult for the Jews. Roman procurators—government officials who collected the empire's taxes—kept increasing the amount of money people owed. Some procurators were keeping part of the money for themselves. The Jews were also denied the right to appoint their own high priests for religious ceremonies. Instead, Rome chose these "holy men" whose loyalty was to Rome, not the Jewish people or even God. Finally, a breaking point came when a Roman procurator started inciting anti-Jewish riots and stealing silver from the Jewish temples. He also crucified hundreds of Jews.

The Jews revolted.

To quell this rebellion, soldiers from Roman's 12th Legion went into Judea to take control. But this military campaign wasn't well-executed, and the zealous Jewish fighters killed many soldiers.

When Roman Emperor Nero heard this news, he flew into a rage—which must've really been something because Nero was already kind of nuts. He had murdered his own mother. And his first wife. And probably his second wife, too. Historians also suspect Nero set fire to the city of Rome—just so he could take credit for rebuilding it!

To deal with this Jewish revolt, Nero dispatched one of his best military leaders, Titus Flavius Vespasian. (His name's a mouthful so we'll just call him Titus.)

Titus Vespasian on his way to subdue the Jewish revolt

Titus had already successfully conquered the island of Britain for Rome. But in Judea, he was up against a very clever rebel leader named Joseph ben Matthias.

To fight Titus and his soldiers, Joseph was training an elite guard of 600 men, 200 horsemen, and 5,000 infantry. He also added about 30,000 conscripts. These men were farmers, merchants, and traders who were forced—or conscripted—to fight in this battle.

Next, Joseph began fortifying a place called Jotapata.

Pronounced "Jo-tah-pah-tah," this city sat atop a high hill. It had stone walls, and the only entrance into the city was from the north, a route that required crossing a dry moat. Joseph realized Jotapata would make an ideal defensive fort for the rebels.

Jotapata defensive wall as it looks today

Titus marched toward Judea with his 60,000 soldiers destroying everything in their path. The Romans burned villages, killed men and women, and took children as slaves. These "scorched-earth" tactics were meant to send a message: Obey Rome or suffer the consequences.

As news spread through Judea, Joseph's conscripts started deserting.

Titus and his army arrived at Jotapata. It was May, in the year 67 AD. The Roman commander set up camp below the hill, then ordered his bowmen to launch a barrage of arrows over Jotapata's walls.

Joseph launched a counterattack.

For the next five days, the attacks and counterattacks continued, until Titus realized these Jews were not going to surrender easily.

Titus decided he needed a way to get over those stone walls. He ordered his men to build a massive platform ramp that would allow his men to breach the wall. But when construction started, Joseph's men climbed onto the city walls and hurled boulders at the Romans. Work came to a standstill.

Titus then launched another heavy barrage of arrows, forcing Joseph's men off the walls.

Joseph countered by sending out striking parties. These raiders would sneak out of Jotapata and inflict hit-and-run tactics on the Romans by stealing their supplies and sabotaging construction on the ramps. Titus, growing more frustrated, finally figured out which routes the raiders were using and closed every one.

Ramp construction continued. So did the Roman barrages of flaming arrows.

But Joseph had his men make shields from animal hides. These shields were fire-resistant because of the moisture—blood and water—in the skins. The Roman's flaming arrows bounced off the shields.

Joseph also raised the city walls by thirty feet, and success-fully launched a nighttime attack that scattered the Romans' front lines further from Jotapata.

Roman Soldiers

Titus decided it was time to launch siege warfare. He would cut off all supplies into Jotapata and starve these rebels into surrender.

But the Jews had counted on a long fight and had stocked Jotapata with plenty of food and weapons. Their real problem was water. The city had only one water well, serving thousands of people inside the walls, during the height of summer. Unless rain came, the city well would soon run dry. Titus was count-ing on that.

To fool the Romans into believing the Jews had plenty of water, Joseph told his men to make a big show of washing their clothes—even though they couldn't actually use water—then hang all the fake laundry on the walls where the Romans could see it. Titus, camping outside the walls with his large army, was growing ever more frustrated.

In reality, however, Joseph's forces were in big trouble. At one point, Joseph said he was going to leave the city to gather reinforcements. But his men suspected him of trying to save his own skin. They placed a guard on him around the clock.

The Romans finished the ramps. Titus moved his war machines close to the city and began launching boulders into Jotapata. The city walls started crumbling.

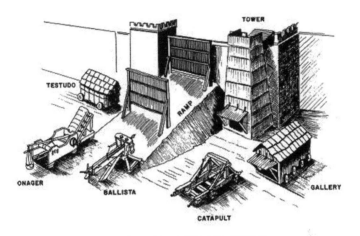

ROMAN SIEGECRAFT AND WORKS
Roman War Machines

As the Romans came closer and closer to breaching the walls, Joseph told his men to collect dry wood and coat it with pitch and sulfur. (Pitch is a kind of tar that burns a long time. Sulfur is a natural flammable compound.) Holding these flaming weapons, the Jews attacked the Romans and set fire to the wooden ramps.

The Romans retreated. But Titus bombarded the city again.

By late June, the Romans had managed to open two gaps in the city wall. Titus sent in his cavalry first wearing full armor, followed by his infantry carrying ladders, backed up by archers and a reserve cavalry force.

Titus had several serious advantages over Joseph. For one thing, he had many more soldiers which allowed him to rotate his forces. This was a Roman tactic in which a commander would continuously move out tired soldiers from a battle and replace them with fresh fighters. And now each pulse of rested warriors caused the exhausted rebels to lose more ground.

And yet, the rebels still refused to surrender.

Joseph decided to try one last trick—something that may have never been used before in warfare. He ordered his men to boil oil and carry it to the top of the walls. As the Romans came up the ramps, the rebels poured the boiling oil on them. The rebels also poured the oil on the ramps, causing the Romans to slip and fall off. Titus' men fled.

But Titus only sent in more soldiers. The fighting continued until darkness fell.

Throughout Judea, news was spreading about this monumental battle at Jotapata, inspiring other rebels to fight against Rome. To quell this uprising, the Romans killed thousands upon thousands of men, women, and children.

Back at Jotapata, Titus now built three towers. Each tower stood fifty feet high, and to keep them from being set on fire like the ramps, iron was laid over the wood. Titus then placed archers inside these towers. Now that they could see over the city walls, the accuracy of their shots grew deadly.

Joseph's men were growing desperate.

To make matters worse, a Jewish deserter ran to Titus and told him about a wall guard who always fell asleep at his post. The next day, as morning fog rolled in, the Romans snuck up on the sleeping guard, killed him, and breached the wall. Taking the rebels by surprise, the Romans slashed their way through Jotapata, killing every person in their path.

Roman coin with Titus on one side, a kneeling Jew on the other. Classical Numismatic Group, Inc.

As the Romans breached the wall, Joseph and some other leaders ran to a secret cave under the city. Joseph wanted to surrender to the Romans, but the men with him refused. The Romans, they said, would torture them to death. Better to take their own lives. However, under Jewish law, suicide was a sin.

Joseph had another idea. Rather than taking their own lives, they would kill each other to avoid the sin of suicide. In order to decide who would kill whom, Joseph convinced the men to draw lots to determine the order of death. In the end, the last two people remained—Joesph and another man. However, instead of one killing the other, they surrendered to the Romans.

Joseph was taken directly to Titus. Before the Roman commander could kill him, Joseph told Titus about a prophecy he had—a holy vision of the future—in which Titus became the supreme ruler of the Roman Empire. After hearing that, Titus decided to spare Joseph's life.

The other rebels were not spared. The Romans killed about 40,000 Jews in the Battle of Jotapata. Another million were killed during the seven-year revolt against Rome. And after finally ending the revolt, Roman soldiers made sure to destroy the holy Jewish temple in Jerusalem.

WHO FOUGHT?

One artist's rendering of Josephus

Joseph ben Matthias fought the Roman army with passion and brilliance. But after the Battle of Jotapata, he was taken as Titus' slave.

But as Joseph's prophecy had predicted, Titus became the emperor of Rome. Titus then granted Joseph his freedom. As a Roman citizen, Joseph ben Matthias changed his name to Josephus.

Josephus wrote many books, including *The Jewish War*, which chronicles the Jewish revolt against the Romans. Most of what we know about the rebellion, and the Battle of Jotapata, comes from Josephus' account—which is why some historians doubt some of the book's truthfulness and accuracy.

For instance, the book claims Joseph survived the battle because God put him in that cave and made sure Joseph picked the right lot to survive. However, historians suspect Joseph plotted the entire surrender scenario, including who would kill whom inside that cave, and that Joseph and his accomplice would survive.

But isn't the process of drawing lots based on random chance? How could Joseph make sure he and his accomplice survived that process?

Here's one theory. Joseph suggested they draw lots. That process probably sounded fair. But mathematically, it's possible to devise a system that beats the odds, if you know the total number of people and how the elimination process will work. For instance, if forty-one people stood in a circle drawing lots, Joseph and his accomplice could stand in the 16th and 31st positions, making sure the counting system skipped over them, leaving them as the last two men standing. This mathematical theory even has a name. It's called a "Josephus problem." (There's a link below to find out more.)

BOOKS

The Jewish Revolt AD 66–74 by Si Sheppard

Roman Legions on the March: Soldiering in the Ancient Roman Army by Susan Provost Beller

INTERNET

You can watch a short summary reenactment of the Romans attacking at Jotapata and the Jewish response—including the attack with boiling oil: www.youtube.com/watch?v=JdLrZhCSWf4

The battle site now—some of the stone walls are still there: www.biblewalks.com/Sites/yodfat.html

Want to know more about that mathematical phenomenon known as the Josephus problem? Check out this short video from Numberphile: www.youtube.com/watch?v=uCsD3ZGzMgE

The Battle of Tours

October 10, 732 AD

CHARLES MARTEL AT TOURS

IF YOU READ MARVEL COMICS, you've probably heard of Thor, the superhero who carries a magical hammer. Thor was based on a character from ancient Viking mythology who also carried a hammer with supernatural powers.

But in real life, there was a "superhero" known as The Hammer. His real name was Charles Martel, and his most famous fight was the Battle of Tours in 732 AD.

Before we get to that battle, we need to cover some background.

The historical era from 500 AD to 1500 AD is known as the Middle Ages. These 1,000 years saw near-constant turmoil. Conflicts and wars erupted across the globe, and drastic shifts altered human civilizations. For instance, the Roman Empire, once seen as invincible, fell to barbarian invaders. New European countries emerged—places we know today as England,

France, Germany, Spain, and Portugal.

Also, in the year 600 AD, a man named Mohammed started a new religion called Islam. Its followers were known as Muslims, and they obeyed a book called the Koran which said everyone should submit to Islam. Anyone who didn't submit to Islam was an "infidel" and deserved to die. During the early Middle Ages, Muslim armies began invading neighboring lands and converting people to Islam. Within a hundred years, Muslim forces gained control of vast areas of the known world.

Look at the map. It shows the "Islamic Caliphate" during the Middle Ages. The map also shows the Byzantine Empire and the Frankish Kingdom. These areas were Catholic, following the teachings of Jesus Christ, but the Islamic Caliphate planned to conquer them.

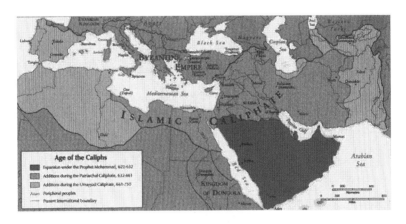

In 732, the Muslim forces were being led by a fierce warrior named Abdul Rahman Al Ghafiqi. He conquered huge parts of the Western world and now was determined to overthrow the Byzantine Empire and the Frankish Kingdom. That would make Islam the dominant religion of Europe instead of Christianity.

Al Ghafiqi's army galloped through what is today's Spain.

His Muslim forces slaughtered infidels and converted the fearful to Islam. Other people—Christians, Jews, pagans—were taken as slaves. Al Ghafiqi's next target was France.

Abdul Rahman Al Ghafiqi

This is where Charles the Hammer comes in.

As a young man, The Hammer grew up studying the military tactics of Alexander the Great. He had learned how to train his forces, how to use terrain for the best advantage in battle, and how to fight in formation like Alexander's Box.

Gathering 30,000 soldiers, Charles the Hammer headed for the city of Tours, France. He suspected this city would be Al Ghafiqi's next major target because it offered great riches to a plundering army.

Since Al Ghafiqi favored straight-on cavalry charges in battle, The Hammer chose high ground outside Tours, hoping to hinder the horse-riding invaders. This elevation also had trees where The Hammer's men could hide. With the Muslim forces outnumbering the Europeans by two to one, The Hammer's men needed the element of surprise.

Fortunately, many of these men had been fighting alongside The Hammer for more than a decade. They also were heavily armored with shields, daggers, swords, lances, and two types of battle axes. The only problem was all that armor could weigh as much as 70 pounds, slowing down their movements, especially against Muslim forces wearing only light cloth tunics and carrying one sword or spear.

Muslim army in France during the Middle Ages

Al Quafiqi marched his forces toward Tours. His army rolled over every opponent. Nobody could stop him.

Then, just outside the city of Tours, The Hammer surprised Al Quafiqi. But instead of an all-out attack, The Hammer withdrew.

This was a clever strategy. Al Ghafiqi wanted to get inside Tours to steal its riches. So The Hammer decided to hold still and frustrate the Muslim commander's desires.

Al Ghafiqi kept sending out his cavalry, but the men on horseback struggled to get up the steep terrain. When they did, they were beaten back by heavily-armored men using a box formation. Moreover, with The Hammer's men hiding in the trees, Al Ghafiqi couldn't tell how many men he was facing.

Al Ghafiqi also faced another enemy at Tours—the weather. It was October and already cold in northern France. Winter would be even colder, and the Muslim forces were wearing only light clothing. They also needed food. But they were surrounded by an unknown enemy who was making it almost impossible to forage for supplies.

The Hammer kept waiting. Militarily, this is called a "defensive attack," forcing the other side to initiate battle.

Al Ghafiqi kept trying to draw the enemy into the open, but The Hammer refused to take the bait, keeping his men hidden, further frustrating the other side.

Finally, after seven days, Al Ghafiqi launched an all-out cavalry charge.

Back then, it was almost impossible for any infantry—the foot soldiers—to survive a heavy cavalry charge of this magnitude. Not only were horses faster than humans, the soldiers riding them had much better positioning to wound or kill during a battle.

With the Muslim soldiers racing for them, The Hammer ordered his men to lock their shields together and create a box formation. Then his heavily armored men extended their swords and other weapons. The cavalry rushed forward. The Hammer's men pushed back, holding their formation. But as the battle continued, some of the Muslim forces broke through and rushed for The Hammer, aiming to kill him and win the fight.

But among The Hammer's many gifts was an ability to adapt on the battlefield. When the Muslim forces broke through, The Hammer reorganized his men. They managed to drive back the enemy.

For some time, the battle continued this way—back and forth—as though neither side would win, when suddenly a rumor broke out. Some of The Hammer's men had snuck away from the battlefield. They were now inside the Muslim camp stealing stuff, including the slaves!

The Muslim cavalry raced back to their tents.

Al Ghafiqi was left on the battlefield.

One Arab historian described the moment this way: "All the host fled before the enemy and many died in the flight."

The Hammer's men launched into the enemy forces and killed Al Ghafiqi.

But even with Al Ghafiqi dead, The Hammer expected another attack the following day. He ordered his men to resume the box formation and wait for a cavalry charge.

When no attack came, The Hammer suspected a trick. He sent out scouts. They returned with a report. The Muslim forces were gone, and they'd fled so quickly their tents were left behind.

The Battle of Tours was over, and The Hammer had saved

the city. He had also protected northern Europe from a Muslim invasion.

Skirmishes still broke out between Muslim and Christian forces, but the Battle of Tours proved to be a critical turning point. After it, the Islamic Caliphate began losing power.

WHO FOUGHT?

Charlemagne

Aside from his legendary military leadership, history doesn't tell us much about Charles the Hammer. We know much more about his grandson, Charlemagne.

Pronounced "Shar-lah-main," Charlemagne also fought Muslim forces throughout Europe. And like his grandfather, Charlemagne was a legendary warrior. His battle victories won so much territory that he created a buffer zone that protected Europe from further invasions.

In many ways, Charlemagne was a heroic figure. He was known for helping the poor.

But he wasn't without controversy.

In 768 AD, Charlemagne placed himself on the Frankish throne, then became King of Italy. In 800, on Christmas day, the Pope named him the first Holy Roman Emperor. To achieve this power, Charlemagne used some strong-arm tactics. He also sometimes spread his Christian faith by his sword—much like the Muslim raiders "converted" infidels by threatening to kill them.

However, Charlemagne encouraged a great revival in Europe and enacted important cultural reforms. His rule helped keep Christianity alive in the western world. Today Charlemagne is referred to as the "Father of Europe."

BOOKS

Warriors of Medieval Times (Heroes & Warriors) by John Matthews and Bob Stewart

Medieval Life: Eyewitness Books by Andrew Langley

Son of Charlemagne by Barbara Willard

The Holy Roman Empire and Charlemagne in World History by Jeff Sypeck

INTERNET

You can find information on the Middle Ages at Ducksters.com: www.ducksters.com/history/middle_ages_timeline.php

Here is an explanation of the Roman Empire turning into the Byzantine Empire: www.ducksters.com/history/middle_ages_byzantine_empire.php

Here is a timeline that begins with the birth of Islam followed by Muslim invasions throughout Europe: www.ducksters.com/history/islam/timeline_islamic_history.php

The Battle of Hastings

October 14, 1066

The Battle of Hastings, by Philip James de Loutherbourg

FOR ANY KING, it's important to name an "heir."

An heir (pronounced "air") is the person who will take over the king's throne after he dies. Throughout history, kings have usually chosen heirs among their sons, brothers, or nephews.

But in the year 1066, the king of England died without making it clear who would be his heir. Supposedly the king was on his deathbed when he named his brother as heir, but not everyone agreed.

That spelled big trouble, because three different men wanted the throne.

One was the dead king's brother, Harold.

The second was King Hardrada of Norway.

And the third was William, the Duke of Normandy, France.

Only Harold lived in England. So if the other two wanted the throne, they would have to invade the country.

Hardrada sailed from Norway to England with 300 ships and more than 15,000 Vikings. Hardrada's forces landed on England's northeast coast. That's when things got even more complicated.

Harold—the dead king's brother and now the self-proclaimed King of England—had another brother. But this brother had been exiled by their dead brother—the former king. The exiled brother was sent to northern England, and now he was offering his men to Hardrada.

Look at the map. It shows Hardrada's invasion route from Norway to northeast England where he gained more fighters, thanks to Harold's exiled brother. Hardrada then marched these men south to fight Harold. Also, see the map's lower half. In the south of England, Harold had another opponent, William the Duke of Normandy, coming from France.

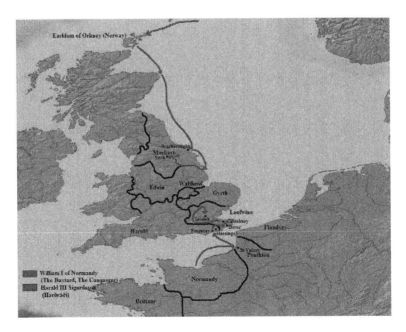

In September 1066, Hardrada's combined forces began fighting Harold's army in northern England. Hardrada's forces were winning the battles. Harold himself wasn't there because he was further south, waiting for William's invasion. But when Harold learned the Vikings invaders were beating his men, he raced north. At the Battle of Stamford Bridge, Harold managed to wipe out Hardrada's combined forces—then killed both his brother and Hardrada. He also destroyed the Viking warships.

But that victory had cost Harold dearly. Many of his men died in the fight. The remaining men were either wounded or exhausted.

At this crucial point, that's when William landed on the southern coast with his invasion force.

Harold raced to confront the invaders, marching his 8,000-man army over more than 200 miles in less than five days. He rested them for another five days, then continued south until he reached an area called Hastings.

That's where William was waiting.

Although Harold and William each had roughly the same size infantry, William had 1,000 archers. Realizing his enemy's advantage, Harold took a defensive position on a hill outside Hastings, using the high ground to protect his army from the archers and cavalry charges.

On the morning of October 14, William ordered his archers to unleash a hailstorm of arrows. The first English soldiers to face those arrows were the Housecarls. Originally Danish, the Housecarls became some of the English's best troops and here they used their shields for protection against the arrows, forcing William's archers to move in closer to hit their targets. And when the archers came near, the English attacked them with spears and axes.

Williams' men retreated.

Medieval battles involved close contact fighting

William next sent out his heavy infantry. Once again, the Housecarls took the upper hand, slashing at the Normans until they retreated.

William then ordered out his cavalry, hoping the horse soldiers could break through the English lines. But the horses struggled to cross the wet and marshy ground, even before having to run uphill to face Harold's forces. And the Housecarls attacked them with their most deadly weapon—double-bladed axes. With one blow, these five-foot long weapons could slice off a horse's head.

Williams' cavalry was forced to retreat.

But as that cavalry rode through its own lines, the center flank opened, giving Harold the perfect opportunity to rush in and take over the battlefield.

But Harold didn't.

Instead, his English infantry charged and broke through their own Housecarls. In the confusion that followed, William fell from his horse. Word shot across the battlefield—William of Normandy was dead! The French began to panic.

And that panic gave Harold *another* opportunity to seize control. But again, he didn't. Some historians wonder if Harold hesitated because an all-out charge might make him lose his defensive position on the hill. But while Harold hesitated, William was able to yank off his helmet and show his men that he was still alive. His troops suddenly rallied. The Nomans charged at the English, forcing them into a retreat.

Throughout the day, The Battle of Hastings moved back and forth, threatening to become a stalemate. Then, as night approached, William decided he couldn't let Harold regroup his army overnight. The English king would only come back stronger the next morning. So William ordered his archers to fire arrows in a high arc, the kind of steep volley that forced the English soldiers into deep defense.

Archers firing arrows over medieval battle

The English raised their shields for protection. This time, William unleashed his infantry at the same time, launching a battle of hand-to-hand combat.

The English lines began to break.

Next William ordered his cavalry into the fight, followed by a group of Norman knights. Altogether, these forces broke through the English line and found Harold. Williams' soldiers killed the King of England. Some records say Harold was already dead, or close to it, having been hit in the eye by an arrow.

Arrow striking King Harold in the eye

The arrow killed Harold. And now that their king was dead, the English soldiers fled into the surrounding woods, hoping to save their lives.

The Battle of Hastings was over, and William had won.

The following day, his Norman soldiers gathered their dead from the battlefield and buried them in a communal grave. The dead English soldiers were left to rot on the ground.

By Christmas Day 1066, William of Normandy was crowned the King of England.

WHO FOUGHT?

Statue of William the Conqueror

At age 8, William suddenly became the Duke of Normandy when his father died on a Christian pilgrimage to Jerusalem.

But since William was an illegitimate son—his mother wasn't married to his father—and since the title of Duke came with land and power, William had plenty of enemies. At one point, these enemies killed Williams' teacher and his guards, hoping to kill him, too. William survived these treacherous years because King Henry I of France helped him.

But the danger continued when William became King of England. Most of the English people were not happy about a Frenchman taking over their country. For one thing, William gave English land to his French followers. The English launched many revolts during Williams' reign. None succeeded.

But William was a successful king in other ways. He ordered a highly detailed census which provided a record of all people and property in England. That census—called The Domesday Book—is a treasure trove of historical information about medieval England. And William changed history itself with his victory at the Battle of Hastings. Ever since that day, every king or queen of England has been a direct descendant of this conquering Frenchman.

BOOKS

King Harold the King: The Story of the Battle of Hastings by
    Helen Hollick

Wulf the Saxon: A Story of the Norman Conquest by G.A. Henty

The Battle of Hastings by Chris Priestly

INTERNET

Awesome Stories has some videos about the battle which also help
    explain which materials historians use to find out what
    happened: www.awesomestories.com/asset/view/Battle-of-
    Hastings-Part-1

The Bayeaux Tapestry shows the Battle of Hastings scene by scene,
    sort of like the medieval version of a graphic novel. You can view
    the tapestry's panels here: www.bayeuxtapestry.org.uk/
    BayeuxContents.htm

MOVIES

The History of Warfare: The Battle of Hastings 1066 (2007) DVD

The Crusades

1090s–1290s

ALTHOUGH CHARLES THE HAMMER stopped the Muslim invasion of Europe, the heated conflict between Christians, Jews, and Muslims continued for centuries.

Around the year 1070, a nomadic tribe of Muslim warriors known as Turks took control of the city of Jerusalem. Jews and Christians alike considered Jerusalem the holy land. The Turks then conquered even more territory, eventually coming within a 100 miles of Constantinople, the capital of the Christian Byzantine Empire.

The Byzantine emperor begged the Catholic pope for help

stopping the Turkish invasion. The pope began encouraging Christians to fight back and seize back control of Jerusalem, even if that meant using military force. This Middle Ages' conflict between Muslims and Christians turned into a long string of epic battles collectively known as The Crusades.

Look at the map. It shows, in simple form, where the Crusades were headed—to Jerusalem (lower right corner). Above Jerusalem, you will see Damascus and Tripoli. Above those two places, see the city of Antioch. That's where our next great battle took place.

THE WORLD OF THE CRUSADERS

The Battle of Antioch

1097

The Siege of Antioch, 15th-century painting

ABOUT 30,000 CHRISTIANS signed up for the First Crusade—peasants, craftsmen, and knights.

Some of these people might've been searching for adventure. Or they hoped to earn fame in battle. But according to most medieval manuscripts and other historical documents, the vast majority of these Crusaders joined because their lives were devoted to Jesus Christ, and they hoped to save Christianity from obliteration by the Muslim forces.

One of the Crusaders' first objectives was to retake the city of Antioch. Once part of the Byzantine Empire, Antioch was now controlled by the Turks.

Inside the city, a Turkish leader named Yaghi Siyan was leading a garrison—a contingent of troops. Hearing the Crusaders were coming, Siyan had called for reinforcements. But before his help could arrive, the Crusaders reached Antioch and the battle broke out.

But the fight soon fell into a stalemate, with neither side gaining the advantage. That was going to be a real problem for both sides, because neither the Crusaders nor the Turks inside Antioch had enough supplies to endure a long battle.

The leader of the Crusaders was a man named Bohemond of Taranto, Italy. As this stalemate continued, a Turkish soldier secretly went to Bohemond and offered to open a section of the stone wall that protected the city. With an opening in the wall, the Crusaders could rush inside Antioch and slaughter the Turks.

But Bohemond knew that the Crusaders would lose the element of surprise if the Turks saw them coming. So the Crusaders came up with a fake-out. They pretended to move in one direction, then circled back, while other soldiers attacked the Turkish guards. Then using ladders, the Crusaders scaled the city wall and raced into Antioch.

Antioch had remained mostly Christian, even under the Turks' rule. Now many of its citizens joined the Crusaders, opening a city gate to let in more forces. During this sudden onslaught, the Turk's leader, Siyan, was killed. Siyan's son grabbed his garrison and pulled the soldiers into a citadel.

Now the Turkish reinforcements arrived, led by a commander named Kerbogha, and it was very bad news for Crusaders inside Antioch—the Turks had them surrounded. No escape was possible.

In the midst of this crisis, a monk named Peter Bartholomew saw a vision of a lance—or spear. Peter said this lance was the very same weapon that the Romans used to stab Jesus Christ as he hung on the cross. If the spear had touched Jesus, then it was holy. Furthermore, Peter said this lance was buried right there, under Antioch's cathedral. The Crusaders quickly dug up the church floor—and found a lance! This discovery filled them with a renewed confidence for this battle.

Discovery of the Holy Lance

Charging from Antioch, the Crusaders attacked the Turkish reinforcements outside the city walls. They also overwhelmed a lightly-armored Turkish cavalry, causing the enemy to break and run.

While this attack was happening, Kerbogha, the leader of the reinforcements, was playing chess. Suddenly he saw his cavalry galloping away and his infantry deserting. Almost in an instant, he had no fighters left.

Kerbogha decided to sue for peace. That means a losing side asks for better terms of surrender.

But that didn't happen.

The Massacre of Antioch by Gustave Dore (circa 1850)

Ignoring the request for surrender, The Crusaders kept attacking.

Kerbogha realized his only chance of survival was a last-minute counterattack. He quickly ordered his men to set fire to a field of grass. He was hoping the billowing smoke would blow into the Crusaders' eyes.

But the fire changed direction.

Now smoke and flames swallowed up the Muslim forces. What remains of Kerbogha's men fell into a full retreat, racing all the way to a Turkish-held city called Mosul. Kerbogha arrived there in disgrace. He had lost Antioch.

Remember Siyan's son, hiding in the citadel with his men? After the crusaders wiped out Kerbogha's forces, they attacked the citadel. And won that, too.

The Battle of Antioch was over.

The Crusaders had taken full control of the city and driven out the Turks. The battle cost them 2,000 men. The Turks lost 10,000 men.

Now the Crusaders resumed their march for Jerusalem. And they eventually recaptured the city. But the victory didn't end this war.

Over the next two hundred years, seven more Crusades would take place. And millions of people died—Christian, Jew, and Muslim alike.

WHO FOUGHT?

Knights Templar

During the Middle Ages, many Christians made a yearly pilgrimage to Jerusalem, their Holy Land. But along the way, the pilgrims were often preyed upon by bandits and highway robbers who stole their money and sometimes killed them.

In the year 1119, a French knight named Hughes de Payens organized a group of monk-knights whose sole job was to protect Christians making the pilgrimage to Jerusalem. To support the effort, the king of Jerusalem gave these knights part of his royal palace, which was located on the ruins of King Solomon's temple. The monk-knights took their name from this location. "Poor Fellow-Soldiers of Christ and of the Temple of Solomon."

Later they were called Knights of the Templar. Or Knights

Templar.

The Templars maintained a high code of conduct. They took vows of chastity (no sex) and poverty (no money). They wore white head coverings called habits, and tunics that were adorned with a large red cross, symbolizing their devotion to Jesus Christ. The Templars' motto was, "Not unto us, O Lord, not unto us, but unto thy Name give glory."

Despite vows of personal poverty, the Templars as a group were quite rich. Among other possessions, they owned an entire fleet of ships, the city of Cypress, and a large treasury, or bank. Kings and nobles borrowed money from the Templars. At the same time, the Templars were highly trained military soldiers. During the Crusades, they were considered among the most highly skilled fighting units.

During the 12th century, Muslim forces re-conquered Jerusalem. The Templars moved their base of operations to Paris, France. But later, a French king decided he didn't like the Templars. Some historians believe the king's animosity was based on the fact that he owed the Templars a lot of money. In any event, in 1307, this king arrested many of the Templars and forced them into false confessions for crimes they didn't commit. The king then burned them at the stake.

BOOKS

Knight (DK Discovery book)

Crusades (DK Discovery book)

Crusades (Graphic Medieval History, 2014) by Gary Jeffrey and Nick Spender

The Boy Knight: A Tale of the Crusades by G. A. Henty

INTERNET

"The First Crusade," is a seven-minute summary on YouTube that includes the Battle of Antioch: www.youtube.com/watch?v= YJfFz836ry4

History.com offers still more videos on different aspects of the Crusades: www.history.com/topics/crusades/videos

MOVIES

The Crescent and the Cross, a History channel DVD about the Crusades

Also, two popular movies refer to the Knights Templar: *Indiana Jones and the Last Crusade* and *National Treasure.*

The Battle of Stirling Bridge

September 11, 1297
Scottish War for Independence

Battle of Stirling Bridge

NOW THAT YOU KNOW about the Battle of Hastings, you know what can happen when a king dies without an heir.

The same is true for queens.

In the year 1290, the Queen of Scotland died. She had *thirteen* children, but she didn't say which one should inherit her throne.

These thirteen siblings—much like Harold and his brothers—fought over who should control Scotland. Finally, they asked the King of England, Edward I, to pick the heir to the

Scottish throne.

Big mistake.

Edward wanted Scotland for himself—Scotland and England share a border—so Edward chose the person who would do whatever Edward wanted. That heir's name was John Balliol. Four years later, the Scottish people realized King John's true nature. They nicknamed him "Toom Tabard"—Scottish for "empty coat." Scotland was in turmoil.

Stirling Bridge (Map)
Scotland is the black landmass sharing its southern border with England below

Meanwhile, England was at war with France. That war was one reason why Edward wanted control of Scotland. He could tax its citizens and use the money to pay for the war.

The Scots had no reason to fight the French, and they didn't appreciate Edward's lackeys taking their hard-earned money to pay for his problem. So the Scottish people revolted, demanding to be free. That revolt launched the Wars of Scottish Independence.

The first battle took place in April 1296. It was a disaster for the Scots as Edward showed no mercy. Now he demanded that Scottish landowners sign the "Raman's Roll," a pledge of allegiance that required paying even more taxes to England.

The future for the Scots looked dim.

But William Wallace would change that.

As a young boy in Scotland, William learned the art of battle—riding horses, wielding swords, foraging for food. William also grew tall—six feet, six inches. Among the people of the Middles Ages, who were often short, William Wallace looked like a giant.

During a rebel skirmish, the English killed William's father and brother. William retaliated by killing an English sheriff. King Edward then named William Wallace an avowed enemy of England, and called for his capture and death.

William Wallace stained glass memorial, Stirling, Scotland

The king's death threat didn't intimidate William Wallace. His great desire was to free Scotland from the English. And the only way to achieve that independence was to defeat King Edward's army in battle.

On September 11, 1297, William Wallace confronted the English army at Stirling Bridge.

Having combined his forces with another rebel leader, William Wallace had about 3,500 men. But no cavalry. And no knights, because most of the Scottish nobles either disliked William Wallace or were too deeply under Edward's control. Wallace's rebels were mostly farmers, merchants, and craftsmen—ordinary Scottish people who wanted to be free from England.

Edward's army, on the other hand, had more than 10,000 soldiers in Scotland alone with another 2,000 cavalry soldiers. The English soldiers were well-trained, carried fine weapons, wore expensive uniforms, and looked down on these ragtag rebels. They were led by a man named John de Warenne.

At Stirling Castle, William Wallace placed his men on high ground where they could see the river down below which was crossed by Stirling Bridge.

Soon after, Warenne and his English forces arrived. But they didn't cross the river for several days. Warenne was certain these crazy rebels would want to negotiate an end to this conflict. Only a fool would try to fight his skillful army that outnumbered them more than three to one.

But every time Warenne called for surrender, William Wallace refused. Finally, Warenne decided to attack.

Stirling Bridge was about nine feet across, just enough room for two horsemen to ride side by side. Horses couldn't ride around the bridge because the land on either side was treacherous—swampy on one side, fast-moving water on the other. With more than 2,000 cavalry soldiers, it was going to take several hours to get that force across the bridge.

Children's book drawing
Artist's rendering of William Wallace

Warenne decided to send his infantry—foot soldiers—in first. Those soldiers started crossing Stirling Bridge at dawn, but Warenne suddenly called them back. He'd overslept, feeling so confident in his easy victory over the rebels. And yet, when Warenne re-sent the infantry across the bridge, he called them back again! This time he said he wanted to give the rebels another chance to surrender.

Warenne sent two priests to talk to William Wallace.

The priests came back with Wallace's reply: "Tell your commander that we are not here to make peace but to do battle, defend ourselves and liberate our kingdom. Let them come on, and we shall prove this in their very beards."

The Battle at Stirling Bridge began.

Warenne had a plan of attack. To cover his infantry as it crossed the bridge, he would send some cavalry upriver. But before he could do this, King Edward's treasurer (the man who keeps track of money) confronted him, complaining that this military campaign had already cost too much money. The treasurer insisted Warenne hurry up and end this silly battle.

Warenne ordered a cavalry charge over Stirling Bridge.

Statue of William Wallace at Edinburgh Castle, Scotland

William Wallace watched with his men as the English riders crossed the bridge.

But he didn't attack.

He waited.

And waited.

He waited until more than 1,000 English cavalry soldiers had crossed the bridge.

Then he attacked.

Charging down hill at full speed, the Scottish rebels screamed war cries and raced straight for the English cavalry, stabbing with long spears, hurling deadly lances, and wielding axes so sharp one blow could decapitate both man and beast.

And now the narrow bridge worked in their favor, much the way that sea channel off Salamis had helped the Greeks. The English had amassed so many cavalry soldiers that they couldn't maneuver away from the rebels or retreat.

The Scottish rebels kept coming, filled with a fury for their enemy and a passion for the homeland. They decimated the English whose knights began jumping off the bridge to save their lives, only to be pulled under water by the weight of their heavy metal armor. Most of them drowned.

Stirling Bridge

Now the Scots charged across the bridge.

Hoping to stop this sudden rout, Warenne ordered his men to set fire to the bridge. But even as the flames rose, the Scots kept coming, racing around the bridge because they had no horses or heavy armor hindered by the swamp and rushing water.

Warenne's forces fell into full retreat.

William Wallace had won the Battle of Stirling Bridge.

This battle was a momentous victory for the Scots. Not only had they killed more than 5,000 English soldiers, they had also proved this rebellion had a fighting chance.

The war for Scottish independence continued for decades. Later, William Wallace was betrayed by his own countrymen, in particular, the Scottish nobles. But in the early 1300s, another charismatic Scot rose to fight England. His name was Robert the Bruce. He won independence for Scotland, and was later named King of Scotland, an independent country.

WHO FOUGHT?

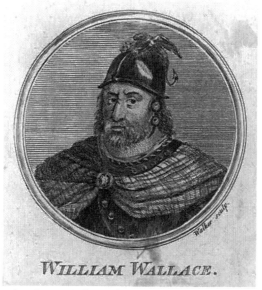

Another artist's rendering of William Wallace

Among the Scottish people, William Wallace was a legendary folk hero. He was the obvious leader of the Scottish rebellion against England and was winning the war. But in 1298, during the Battle of Falkirk, Wallace's men suddenly refused to take his orders. Later it was revealed that before the battle, they had decided to betray him. More than 15,000 Scottish rebels died in that battle.

Wallace then fled to France, hoping the French king would

support his fight against the English—after all, France was at war with England, too. The French king voiced his support but offered no help on the battlefield.

Returning to Scotland, William Wallace decided to use guerrilla warfare tactics. Hiding in the woods, his men continually caught the English soldiers by surprise. The guerrilla tactics were so effective that King Edward increased the bounty—or reward—for William Wallace's head.

The bait of money worked.

In 1305, one of Wallace's close "friends" turned him over to the English.

Wallace was tried in London for treason without being given a lawyer or a jury.

The English court also refused to let him speak during his trial. However, at one point, when he was accused of being a traitor, Wallace replied, "I could not be a traitor to Edward, for I was never his subject."

Found guilty of treason, William Wallace was stripped naked, wrapped in oxhide, and dragged four miles by horses. He was still alive. Next, he was hanged, but at the last moment, his noose was loosened to keep him alive. The English then cut off his testicles, dug out his bowels and organs, and burned these parts in front of him—while Wallace was still alive.

Finally, William Wallace was beheaded.

His head was preserved in tar and placed on a spike atop London Bridge. His body was cut into four parts and sent to various towns for display, warning anyone who even considered disobeying King Edward.

BOOKS

In Freedom's Cause: A Story of Wallace and Bruce (Dover Children's Classics) by G. A. Henty

William Wallace and All That by Allan Burnett

Robert the Bruce and All That by Allan Burnett

The Story Of Scotland by Richard Brassey

INTERNET

Ten facts about William Wallace: learnodo-newtonic.com/william-wallace-interesting-facts

MOVIES

Braveheart

The Siege of Vienna

1529

THE BATTLES WITHIN THE CRUSADES lasted for centuries. But it still didn't stop the Turks from conquering new territory in the west. By the 1500s, the Turk's Ottoman Empire was so large and powerful that it posed a direct threat to the countries of Europe.

Once again, war would break out between the religions of Islam and Christianity.

But this time, the Turks were led by one of history's most cunning and brilliant warriors, Suleiman II.

Suleiman had a massive military—about 120,000 infantry, additional artillery and cavalry soldiers, and another 200,000 support personnel. He also had 90,000 war camels. These animals carried men, supplies, and equipment such as Suleiman's 500 cannons. Suleiman also had a special elite force known as Janissaries. When the Ottoman Turks captured new territory, they would sometimes allow the Christians and Jews living there to continue to practice their religion—provided those people paid a tax to the Turks. However, if those people couldn't pay the fee, the Turks demanded a "blood tribute." Scouring the empire, they would find the strongest Christian boys and make them slaves heavily indoctrinated in Islam. They were also prohibited from marrying and could only devote their loyalty to the sultan. These young men grew up to become Janissary soldiers, among the Turk's most fanatical fighters.

In 1529, Suleiman marched this powerful military force over the mountains of Europe and into Austria. His sights were set on the city of Vienna. The city was wealthy, and it contained some of the most impressive Christian churches in all of Europe.

The Turks were united under their call for "jihad," or holy war, against Christianity. But the Europeans weren't as united. In the early 1500s, for instance, Spain, France, and Germany were all fighting each other—in Italy. When Suleiman and his forces arrived, it would force the Europeans to fight a two-pronged war, stretching their resources and weakening their armies.

Ottoman warriors

Suleiman seemed to have everything he needed for victory—soldiers, equipment, and a weakened enemy.

There was just one problem. He couldn't control the weather.

For several weeks, heavy rain fell in northern Europe, washing away entire bridges. Roads flooded, turning to mud so sticky that thousands of camels broke their legs in it and died.

"It rained so hard," wrote Suleiman's secretary, "that many people drowned in the river."

But the bad weather was a great blessing for Vienna. Without all his camels to carry his equipment, Suleiman was forced to abandon 200 heavy cannons before he reached the city. However, his massive force was still coming, and Vienna was gripped with fear. Austria's King Ferdinand asked his brother, the emperor of Germany, for help, but his brother had his own troubles fighting the French in Italy. Instead, Vienna found help from an unlikely soldier. His name was Nicolas Graf von Salm and he was seventy years old—a very old man in the

1500s when most people didn't live past age sixty.

Von Salm immediately started preparing Vienna for its battle against Suleiman.

Drawing from 1529 showing Ottomans camped outside Vienna

First, von Salm sent away all the women and children. Next, he reinforced Vienna's city walls. After that, he dug up the local paving stones to build a second wall, stripped the city's rooftops of all flammable wooden shingles, and destroyed most of the buildings outside the city, ensuring the Turks would have no cover when they arrived. Inside the city, he placed a garrison of men that included 23,000 infantry soldiers, 2,000 cavalry, and 75 cannons.

Vienna's location offered several natural defenses. To the north, the Danube River blocked entrance into the city. Another waterway protected the city's eastern side. That meant von Salm only needed to defend the walls to the south and west. For his command post, he chose a medieval church that was the highest point in Vienna. But for the battle itself, he transferred leadership to a younger man, Duke Frederick. The duke had recently arrived in Vienna with about 100 Landsknecht— German mercenaries trained to use long-pike weapons. The duke also brought 700 Spaniards armed with a new type of musket.

German Landsknecht mercenaries, circa 1529

The Turks' weapons included crescent-shaped bows with so much driving force the arrows could penetrate chain mail armor. They also carried a curved sword called a scimitar. For guns, Suleiman's men were using match-lock muskets, which had a mechanical device that ignited gunpowder.

In late September 1529, Suleiman's Ottoman army arrived outside Vienna. The heavy rains had killed a good portion of his men and camels, and now a fevered illness further handi-capped his troops. However, Suleiman still believed this fight for Vienna would be a quick battle. After all, he'd beaten much tougher opponents. And most of Europe's soldiers were fighting far away to the south in Italy. They couldn't help Vienna.

Suleiman's first sent a courier into the city. His message was simple. "Surrender now and you will all be spared. If you resist, the place will be razed to the ground and all therein put to the sword."

Von Salm sent the courier back to Suleiman—with no reply.

The next day, Suleiman's 300 Turkish cannons opened fire on Vienna. But Vienna's reinforced walls held, in part because Suleiman had left behind his heaviest and most powerful cannons, stuck in the mud.

Following the cannon bombardment, the Austrians executed a quick cavalry charge. They managed to overrun two Turkish gun emplacements, cut down the crews, and ride safely back into the city.

Suleiman replied with more bombardments.

Then, on October 1, a Turkish engineer snuck into the city. He may have been a Janissary soldier who had kept his original faith because he claimed to be a Christian, and he wanted to warn the Austrian forces that Suleiman's bombardments were just a ploy. The real attack was still coming—from underground.

One artist's vision of siege bombardment, illustrated in the year 1484

While the Turks fired cannons on Vienna, they were also digging tunnels under the city walls and filling the cavities with gunpowder. Suleiman planned to detonate the gunpowder, blowing up Vienna and creating so much chaos his men could quickly take control of the city.

After hearing about these tunnels, von Salm devised an alarm system. He placed buckets of water and drums of dried peas on top of the areas where the Muslims were digging. Any underground disturbances would ripple the water and rattle the peas. Then guards could alert von Salm. The city's defenders would then dig down and take the Turks by surprise.

The plan worked. Von Salm's men stopped every Turkish tunnel—until one fateful day.

On October 5, an explosion tore open the city wall. The Turks rushed into the city.

The Landsknecht mercenaries with their twelve-foot pikes fought back, while another explosion ripped open a city gate. The Turks' Janissary soldiers raced into Vienna, and were confronted by the Spaniards wielding their new firearm—a wheel-lock musket that could fire much faster than any guns among the Turks. The defenders pushed the Turks out of the city.

Ottoman archer

Now von Salm added another tactic to the battle. He placed heavy cannons on the city's rooftops and fired down on the Ottoman camps outside the city walls.

Then, on October 11, the rain returned. More Turkish camels died, and thousands more men fell sick with illnesses. Suleiman's food supplies began to run low. The Turkish leader hadn't expected a long battle at Vienna. Now he needed to launch an all-out attack, defeat the enemy, and get the supplies inside the city.

His plan was to send in novice soldiers first. After these soldiers exhausted the city's defenders, he would send in his experienced men to destroy the weakened enemy.

The attack began on October 14.

Suleiman's two main targets were the Corinthian gate and a section of wall known as the Berg. Once again, he set off underground mine explosions but only one blast worked effectively. And when the novice Turks ran into the city, the German mercenaries wiped them out. The experienced Turkish soldiers raced in next, only to be struck by musket and cannon fire. Suleiman lost about 20,000 soldiers.

That night, under cover of darkness, Suleiman escaped Vienna with his remaining men and camels. He could not take Vienna.

The Battle of Vienna not only stopped the Turk's best commander, it also halted the Ottoman Empire's invasion of northern Europe.

For a while.

About 150 years later, in 1683, the Turks made another attempt to take Vienna. On their way to the city, they trounced entire villages, killing, raping, and taking captives. As the 150,000 Muslim soldiers closed in on Vienna, Austria's King

Leopold fled with most of the city's citizens, leaving behind only a small garrison of 11,000 soldiers and 5,000 citizen volunteers.

Ottoman Turks fighting outside Vienna, 1683

Following von Salm's example, the Austrians once again destroyed buildings outside the city walls, locked the city gates, and prepared for another epic battle.

The Turks fired on Vienna's walls for two solid months.

However, this time, European forces were united under the Holy Roman Empire and were no longer fighting among themselves in Italy. Also, just north of the city, 80,000 Austrian and Polish soldiers launched one of history's largest cavalry charges, attacking the Turks outside Vienna and chasing them out of the country.

This second battle for Vienna marked a closing to the 300-year struggle between the Ottoman Empire and the Holy Roman Empire. Soon after the battle, the Ottoman Empire began to shrink in both size and power.

WHO FOUGHT?

Suleiman

Sultan Suleiman II was known among his people as "The Law Giver."

As sultan, he lived in great luxury. The royal courts, which housed as many as 9,000 people, were opulent palaces. The water fountains sprayed in unison with music. The goldfish had jewels attached to their fins. Suleiman himself wore a broad oval turban adorned with diamonds and peacock feathers. Nothing was too good for the sultan of the Ottoman Empire.

Suleiman rule was a golden age for the empire. He oversaw important developments in literature, mathematics, art, and architecture. But at the same time, Suleiman was an ambitious warlord who studied the military tactics of Alexander the Great. And like Alexander, Suleiman enjoyed leading his men into battle on horseback. During his reign, he conquered large parts of the Middle East, North Africa, and Europe.

Suleiman was married to a Christian woman who had converted to Islam. They had many sons, but Suleiman executed most of them, worried over their threat to his power.

After Suleiman's death in 1566, the Ottoman Empire never regained its golden age.

BOOKS

Days of Danger by Fritz Habeck

Vienna 1683: Christian Europe Repels the Ottomans by Simon Millar

INTERNET

YouTube offers several historical documentaries and re-enactments of the Battle of Vienna, 1529.

Here is an eight-minute video: www.youtube.com/watch?v= Mfiri-0QUkE

And a longer documentary: www.youtube.com/watch?v= pPXDgUrg5E8

The Spanish Armada Invasion of England

1588

English ships fighting the Spanish Armada in 1588.

DURING THE MIDDLE AGES, conflict and turmoil remained almost constant. Battles and wars regularly broke out among France, England, Spain, Portugal, Italy, and Germany.

But one of the most significant conflicts was between England and Spain.

It started with gold.

In 1568, some Spanish ships were docked near England. These ships were carrying gold, and England's Queen Elizabeth I decided to seize it. Spain, naturally, wanted its gold back.

But Elizabeth refused to return it. So Spain retaliated by seizing all property inside its own borders that belonged to the English.

At this point, neither Spain nor England wanted an all-out war. England was struggling financially and had no navy that could confront Spanish ships. Instead, England had "privateers." Also called Buccaneers, these sailors were private citizens given official powers by Queen Elizabeth.

Spain, on the other hand, had the world's most powerful navy, known as the Spanish Armada. These ships, called galleons, ruled the oceans, sailing around the globe, helping Spain conquer vast parts of the world—from Central and South America, to Africa, Asia, and islands in the Caribbean. Spanish forces took treasures from these places, often by force, then sailed back to their homeland.

But Queen Elizabeth suspected that King Philip of Spain wanted to invade her country, too. So she began building a real navy, hoping England would one day have the kind of ships that could fight the Spanish Armada.

Elizabeth I. Notice the ships at war, while the queen rests her hand on the world.

But until that naval fleet was ready, Elizabeth gave the privateers the power to demand money from anyone committing an "offense" against England. Sometimes the privateers invented offenses, and sometimes they attacked the Spanish galleons, stealing their great treasures.

King Philip was furious.

But Elizabeth was going to provoke him even further.

Philip wanted control of the Netherlands, a wealthy country north of England. Back then, the Netherlands was suffering through a civil war. Philip sent Spanish soldiers there, throwing his support to one side of the war. Elizabeth followed suit, sending 4,000 English soldiers—to support the other side.

Now Philip decided it was time to invade England.

His plan included two waves of attack. The first wave, led by the Duke of Medina, would come from his famous Armada, with the galleons sailing from Spain to England. The second wave would come from the Netherlands, where ships commanded by Spain's Duke of Parma would sail down to England. The combined forces would seize control of the southern ports, then conquer England's largest city, London.

Look at the map. Starting at the far left bottom, follow the upward arrow. That's the route taken by the Spanish Armada sailing to England. (We'll get to the other arrows in a moment).

See where the Armada turned sharply east (to the right) at Plymouth. That waterway separating England and France is known as the English Channel.

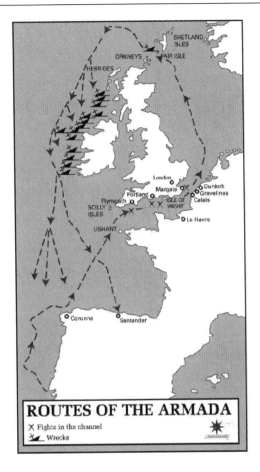

ROUTES OF THE ARMADA

X Fights in the channel
Wrecks

In late May 1588, one hundred and thirty Spanish galleons sailed for England, armed with 8,000 sailors, thousands of guns and cannons, and 3,000 servants whose job was to take care of the crews, especially the officers.

In battle, the galleons used tactics similar to ancient triremes—ramming into an enemy ship then boarding. The galleons would also sail close enough to an enemy ship that the sailors could throw ropes with grappling hooks, latch onto the enemy's rails, and swing themselves over, landing on the deck for close-combat fighting that often involved swords and daggers.

These galleons were enormous vessels, which was an advantage for ramming tactics. But when it came to quick maneuvers, the galleons struggled. Another disadvantage was their cannons. These guns had terrible recoil—when fired, they bucked backward—so the Spaniards mounted them on wheeled platforms. When the cannon fired, it rolled backward. Then the sailors would roll it back into position and reload. That repositioning process slowed down the ship's firing speed.

Spanish galleon

Now the Armada was sailing for England, but unfortunately for Philip, Elizabeth's new navy was ready. Her English fleet included twenty-five modern "race built" ships—much smaller than the galleons—and equipped with heavy cannons for long-range fighting. The long-range element was crucial. The English ships could fire on the galleons without getting close enough to be rammed or boarded. Also, the English cannons were mounted on better carriages that allowed for quicker firing and reloading.

On July 30, 1588, the Spanish Armada entered the English Channel. Almost immediately, the sailors spied an opening at the port city of Plymouth, ideal for landing invasion troops. But the Duke of Medina chose to stick to Philip's orders, which directed the Armada to keep sailing through the English Channel and combine with the ships from the Netherlands. Philip's plan had some sound reasoning.

"I must warn you," Philip wrote to his naval commanders, "that the enemies intention will be to fight at long distance, on account of his advantage in artillery…. The aim of our men, on the contrary; must be to bring him to close quarters and grapple with the weapons they hold in their hands: and you will have to be very careful to carry this out."

But the next day, the Armada found a new enemy—the English Channel.

Spanish sailors were not familiar with the North Atlantic tides and currents or the area's brutal storms. But now all these natural forces were pinning the large ships against the English coastlines.

And the English ships were racing toward the trapped Armada.

English ships and Spanish Armada in battle
August 1588

For naval defense, the Duke of Medina shifted his galleons into a crescent-shaped formation. Usually that formation provided an excellent defensive position because only ships on the wings would be exposed to direct attack. But the English ships quickly countered, adjusting their positions, too, and began broadside strikes—aiming their long-range cannon fire at the broadsides of the galleons.

The battle began.

Commanders yelled orders. Cannons boomed. Smoke choked the air.

But neither side was doing much damage to the other. The English ships were too far away for the Spanish cannons, and the massive galleons were strong enough to withstand the English cannon fire.

Now the swift English ships swept around the Armada, attacking from a rear position. The English also started concentrating their fire, aiming for one ship at a time. When the cannonballs hit the *San Salvador,* the galleon caught fire, exploded, and sank, taking down the Armada's paymaster, the man in charge of paying salaries to the sailors.

King Philip II of Spain

As the Duke of Medina watched these speedy English ships outsmarting his tactics, he decided to disengage from the battle. He ordered his fleet to sail for a friendly port and resupply. The English ships tried to intercept the galleons, but failed.

Now the duke began reorganizing for the next attack.

However, the next day no wind blew across the water. These ships couldn't sail without wind. But the day after, the wind picked up and the battle resumed. Once again both sides were firing on the other, but neither was doing much damage. In fact, the English fired so frequently on the Armada that they ran low on ammunition. Placing the privateers in charge of holding off the galleons, the English race ships left the battle-field to get more ammo.

The duke saw this as his chance to escape.

The galleons took off.

More than 100 English ships pursued them, prompting the duke to change his plan.

Anchoring near the port of Calais, France—the narrowest part of the English Channel—the duke readied his fleet to ram and board the English ships.

That's when bad news arrived.

That second fleet King Philip was sending from the Netherlands? It wouldn't arrive for another two weeks.

The English sailors now took advantage of the anchored galleons. They loaded up old vessels with wood and other flammable debris, lighted them, and sent the ships across the water—giant flaming torches headed straight for the big wooden galleons.

The duke ordered the Armada to cut anchor and flee.

It was a disorganized retreat, completely out of formation, with the English still firing on them. The Spanish fleet was forced to sailing north, instead of south to Spain. (On the map, follow those arrowed lines through the English Channel). It was a treacherous escape. As the galleon kept moving north, Atlantic storms battered the ships. Supplies ran low. More ships wrecked off the coasts of Scotland and Ireland. The ships didn't make it back to Spain until October. Half of the original fleet was gone. And 15,000 men were dead.

The Spanish invasion had failed.

And now the Armada was no longer the world's most powerful navy. Instead, Queen Elizabeth's navy was going to rule the high seas for many years to come. Her smaller, faster ships also changed tactics and strategies in naval warfare. Gone were the days of ramming, boarding, and close-quarter fighting. Naval battles would now be won by sleeker vessels equipped with long-range weapons.

The era of modern warfare had begun.

WHO FOUGHT?

Sir Francis Drake

Sir Francis Drake was England's second-in-command during this battle with the Spanish Armada. Drake was also partly responsible for those fire ships that forced the Armada to flee.

Many of Drake's exploits were the stuff of legend.

In 1577, he circumnavigated the globe—meaning sailed around the world—and was probably the first Englishman to see the Pacific Ocean. Although basically a pirate, he had official standing, thanks to Queen Elizabeth. The English people considered Drake a national hero.

But Spain considered him a villain and nicknamed him *El Draque.*

Drake was known for stealing loot from Spanish ships. In fact, his crews sometimes took so much gold from the galleons that the weight threatened to sink the English ships. So Drake and his men would sometimes divide the spoils, bury part of it, and come back later to dig it up. Several legends claim some of the buried treasure is still in the ground.

King Philip wanted Drake dead. He offered a massive reward. Today the amount would be equivalent to four million dollars.

Spanish gunners managed to fire a cannonball at Drake's ship that went through his cabin. Drake survived the attack, but later died from a tropical disease. However, before his death, he made his funeral wishes known. Dressed in full armor, his body was placed inside a lead coffin and buried at sea.

Deep sea divers continue to search for Sir Francis Drake's coffin.

BOOKS

Elizabeth I and the Spanish Armada (Stories From History) by Colin Hynson

Defeat of the Spanish Armada (How Do We Know About?) by Deborah Fox

Who Was Queen Elizabeth? by June Eding and Nancy Harrison

Sir Francis Drake: Slave Trader and Pirate (Wicked History) by Charles Nick

Under Drake's Flag (A Tale of the Spanish Main): And Other Stories by G.A. Henty

INTERNET

Battlefield Britain's presentation on the Spanish Armada's attempted invasion of England: www.youtube.com/watch?v=Jl3stf20X10

MOVIES

The Seahawk (1940) Errol Flynn stars as an English privateer defending his nation on the eve of the Spanish Armada's invasion.

AFTERWORD

I HOPE YOU ENJOYED READING about these amazing battles from history. But there is much more to discover about them. Go find out!

And if you'd like to read about other battles, there are other books in this series, listed below.

Don't hesitate to drop me a note. You can reach me through my website, www.greatbattlesforboys.com for boys. Sign up for my newsletter to learn of new releases. You can also contact me through Facebook at www.facebook.com/GreatBattles

MORE BOOKS IN THE
GREAT BATTLES FOR BOYS SERIES

Bunker Hill to WWI

The Civil War

World War II in Europe

World War II in the Pacific

Find them at www.amazon.com/Joe-Giorello/e/B00NTBFSB8